# *The* Grandmother BOOK

# The Grandmother BOOK

Betty Southard
and
Jan Stoop

THOMAS NELSON PUBLISHERS
Nashville

*We lovingly dedicate this book*
*to our grandchildren,*
*Timothy, Toria, Elizabeth, David,*
*Michelle, and Colleen.*

Published in Nashville, Tennessee, by Thomas Nelson, Inc.,

Scripture quotations are from the NEW KING JAMES VERSION of the Bible. Copyright © 1979, 1980, 1982, Thomas Nelson, Inc., Publishers.

Scripture quotations taken from the HOLY BIBLE: NEW INTERNATIONAL VERSION® are marked (NIV) in the text. Copyright © 1973, 1978, 1984 by International Bible Society. Used by permission of Zondervan Publishing House. All rights reserved.

**Library of Congress Cataloging-in-Publication Data**

Southard, Betty.
    The grandmother book / by Betty Southard. Jan Stoop.
      p. cm.
  ISBN 0-8407-7747-7
  1. Grandmothers—United States.   2. Grandparenting—United States.
  I. Stoop, Jan.  II. Title.
  HQ759.9.S68   1993
  306.874'5—dc20              92-40955
                                  CIP

Printed in the United States of America.
1 2 3 4 5 6 7 — 97 96 95 94 93

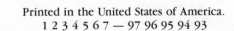

# Contents

# *Acknowledgments*

We want to thank all the wonderful grandmas and grandchildren who took time out from their busy lives to participate in our survey and to those who contributed stories. A special thanks to grandmas who came to our grandmothers meeting at the Crystal Cathedral and to Dainie Clymer for planning and helping us put together the grandmothers meeting.

A big thank you to Janet Thoma for her encouragement all along the way and for her excitement about our subject, and to Kay Strom, who helped integrate our two styles of writing.

And to our very own unique grandparents and special parents we give our thanks, for they gave us a gracious, loving model to show us what grandparenting is all about.

*Introduction*

# The Gift of a Grandbaby

*E*ven though we had both been told again and again how special it was to be a grandma, neither of us was prepared for the flood of emotions we felt as we held our own first tiny grandbaby. What love! What overwhelming joy! But there were unexpected emotions as well— uncertainty and concern—and there were great expectations to be met. This grandmother job wasn't going to be easy!

We also felt an overwhelming sense of responsibility. We desperately wanted to be the kind of grandmas who make a positive difference in the lives of their grandchildren. But as time went on, we were faced with aspects of grandmothering we hadn't planned on, times when sorrow outweighed the joy, times when we were tempted to say, "Who needs this?" and throw ourselves into our own "busyness" rather than face the frustrations of grandmothering.

"Are we the only grandmas who feel this way?" we asked each other. "Are we the only ones who just can't seem to get it all together?"

Apparently not. We've talked to enough other grand-mothers to know these times are tough for everyone. Chil-dren today are growing up in a stress-filled world. Many live in families that are barely hanging together. Others are struggling to cope with families that have already disinte-grated. Little ones need someone willing to champion their causes and fill the empty spaces in their young hearts and lives. They need someone in addition to their parents to be there for them, someone to love and encourage and accept them.

Even healthy, caring moms and dads who do their best for their children need help. No parent can be everything a child needs. Many times the energy required for parent-ing is just too great, especially when parents are depleted and needy themselves. One grandmother described grandparenting as "standing in the gap." What a wonder-ful concept! Our grandchildren need gap fillers.

Do you sometimes feel your grandmothering skills could stand some strengthening? Do you need help in suc-cessfully sharing yourself and your love with your grand-children? Are you frustrated with your attempts to "stand in the gap"? Are you convinced you have a great deal to give, yet are at a loss about *how* to give it? Well, Grandma, welcome to the club.

You may be one of the many grandmothers who, be-cause your efforts are unappreciated or resented, has backed away from involvement in your grandchildren's lives. Or you may feel you are too young to be thrust into this role. Your time may be limited because you have a full-time job, or maybe you have children of your own still at home. Maybe you live hundreds of miles away from those special grandchildren. Or perhaps you feel frustrated, an-gry, or crushed by the attitudes or behavior of your own children. Maybe you've even struggled with a court system that refuses to hear your side.

It may be that you are just beginning to embrace the role of grandmother. Although you don't quite know what to expect, you are determined to be the very best grandma you can possibly be.

Whatever your grandmothering situation, this book was written for you. From a survey we conducted, we have accumulated responses and stories from countless women across the United States (and some from out of the country as well). We have also drawn upon experts in the fields of relationships and personalities for advice and guidance. And we have pulled from our own experiences as grandmothers. Jan, the mother of three sons, has two granddaughters, ages eight and two. Betty, the mother of three daughters, has four grandchildren who range in age from nine to two years old, and two more are on the way. We know how you feel, Grandma. We are right in there with you!

Grandmothering is far more than just picnics in the park or playing special games or sending gifts through the mail. Successful grandmothering takes time and effort. It takes commitment—to love, to pray, to be available, and to make sure each grandchild knows without a shadow of a doubt that he or she is valued as a precious treasure.

One wise grandmother told us, "Grandmothering is about praying and playing."

It is our sincere hope that this book will be an encouragement to you, that it will minister to you and give you help and hope as you work through the tough times. Most of all, it is our prayer that you will experience the incomparable joy of making a difference in the life of each of your precious grandchildren!

*Part 1*

*The Joys of*
*Grandmothering*

# Chapter 1

﹏

# *Happiness Is Being a Grandmother*

Jan sank into the seat next to her husband on a nearly filled airplane. The three seats next to her were empty, and she hoped they would stay that way. After an exhausting two weeks in Florida, she was looking forward to relaxing all the way to California. When the flight attendant began closing the overhead bins in preparation for takeoff, Jan spread out for a comfortable flight.

Just as the door was being closed, an older couple rushed in with a little girl about five years old. They hurried down the aisle, dragging many more than their allotted number of carryons. When they reached the seats next to Jan, they stuffed their belongings and souvenirs into the already-filled storage bins and under and all around their seats. The little girl sat down between the adults she called Grandma and Grandpa, carefully balancing her Disney tote bag on her lap.

"Get that seat belt on," Grandpa ordered the child. "Do you want to get sucked out of the plane?"

The little girl, eyes wide, quickly fastened her seat belt. Grandma began nervously talking about how much she hated to fly. "If something happens to this plane, nobody will get off alive!" she fretted.

When Grandpa told her to hush, she turned on him. "If you hadn't gotten us to the airport late, I wouldn't be so nervous. Why can't you ever plan ahead? I tell you and tell you, but you refuse to change!"

Grandpa ignored her. He had picked up a magazine and was already engrossed in it.

Not long after takeoff, the airplane encountered a bit of turbulence and began to bounce around. Grandma let out one four-letter word after another, her voice loud enough to be heard several rows away.

"Don't talk like that in front of Jenny!" Grandpa hissed.

Grandma had a few choice things to say to Grandpa too. For three and a half hours, Grandma and Grandpa's ongoing bickering was interspersed with admonitions to little Jenny: "Don't color out of the lines." "Don't touch that button or the stewardess will come and you'll be in big trouble."

*Poor little Jenny,* Jan remembers thinking. *She's sitting up straight and trying not to wiggle and doing her best to find something to do that will get the approval of Grandma and Grandpa, something that won't result in another scolding or threat.*

Long after the plane landed in Los Angeles, the little girl was still on Jan's mind. With grandparents like that, what were Jenny's parents like? What kind of home was she going back to? Did she ever get a chance to be a little child and wiggle in her seat and color outside the lines? Did she know what it was like to have the important adults in her life accept and love her? Was she ever able to make her grandparents happy?

But Jan was also thinking about the grandparents. What

kind of people were they? How did they really feel about Jenny? What had their own grandparents been like? Did they ever talk to other grandparents about their grandparenting role? Did they ever share their uncertainties, frustrations, and fears with anyone?

These grandparents probably really did love their little granddaughter. After all, they had taken her all the way across the country to Disney World, and they had obviously spent a great deal of money to make it a special event. So why were they having so much trouble demonstrating their love and acceptance?

Most grandparents truly do want to do a good job of grandparenting. They want to be able to give what their grandchildren need from them—physically, emotionally, and materially. But many grandparents aren't able to be all they want to be or all they could be. Like Jenny's grandparents, their honest attempts can end up with anger, frustration, misunderstandings, and hurt feelings on all sides.

Sometimes we allow our feelings to create barriers that keep us from being the grandmothers we would like to be.

## When Barriers Arise

We grandmothers are much more than just the parents of parents. We are people in our own right who need to feel loved and accepted too. We have our own issues to work out. And when we get frustrated and bogged down, most of us tend to react to our pain and confusion by pulling away from other people, even from our own grandchildren. As we talked with women about grandparenting, we found three things repeatedly cited as barriers to a grandmother's happiness with her grandchildren.

## Barrier 1: Frustration about the Grandmother's Role

Many women claim that as grandmothers, they are able to see things more clearly than when they were mothers. Along with freedom from the responsibility of being a parent, they say, comes the ability to shift their priorities. They are right. But now the question is, What are you going to do with this new perspective? If you don't know what's expected of you, your frustration can easily become a barrier that causes you to become an intrusive grandmother. Take time, instead, to explore ways to fulfill your grandma role appropriately.

## Barrier 2: The Aging Process

For other grandmothers, the aging process itself is the barrier. These grandmas are struggling to adjust to and accept the physical and emotional changes in their own lives. A few are so convinced the word *grandmother* is synonymous with old age, they resist both the name and the role.

Many of us have experienced the realization that some of the things we had planned on and hoped for will never be. The surprising thing to us was the number of grandmothers who also told of repeated bouts of depression and of their inability to cope physically with all that this stage of life brings.

## Barrier 3: Personality Differences

Another barrier we encountered was the misunderstandings that come from personality differences. Not all grandmothers operate the same way. There are different styles of grandparenting, just as there are different styles of parenting. Which is your style? (We'll help you answer that question in Chapter 5.) How does your grandparenting style fit in with your children's parenting styles? How does it fit in with each of your grandchildren and his or her specific needs?

While it's important that you be free to grandparent according to your own style, differences do cause misunderstandings, and they set us up for situations that can be perceived as threatening to our children and our grandchildren as well as to ourselves. Understanding and accepting the different personalities at work within our relationships will help us recognize our limits as well as our gifts.

### How Am I Doing as a Grandma?

Ultimately, the real questions each of us must face are personal ones: How am I doing as a grandma? Do I honestly believe grandmothers can make a difference? Am I making a difference by providing a safe haven where my grandchildren can drop any facades and be themselves? Or am I allowing the internal stresses of my own life to weigh so heavily on me that I am not able to be an effective grandmother?

"That episode with Jenny and her grandparents made a real impression on me," Jan recalled, "so I talked it over with Betty, my friend and prayer partner. I told her I wanted to be a great grandma for my grandchildren and I wanted to help other grandmothers too. She had been thinking the same thing."

That's how it all started. Together we began to talk and pray, and we planned ways we grandmothers could really make a difference in the lives of our grandchildren. Understanding that children need to know there is someone, beyond their parents, who loves them in a very special way, we began to search for practical ideas to help grandmothers stand in the gaps of their grandchildren's lives.

You may be saying, "But my grandchildren are blessed with loving parents who are doing a great job of giving them what they need." Maybe so. But however adequate a parent's love, there is still a role for a grandmother's love too; our love complements the love and understanding our grandchildren get from their parents.

## Can We Really Make a Difference?

Just how much of a difference do grandparents actually make? To find out, we went straight to the true experts in the field—women who are grandmothers, and men and women who told of experiences with their grandmothers. Besides talking and listening, we asked hundreds of women nationwide to help us by answering a questionnaire surveying their experiences. We asked about their grandparenting style and about their feelings toward and relationships with their grandchildren. We also asked them to write what they remembered most about their own grandmothers, what was special about them, and what influence their grandmothers had on their lives.

Women who had not had a living grandparent expressed a real sense of loss. Many told of the envy they had felt as children for their friends who had grandmothers and grandfathers. Almost universally, they were convinced they had missed out on something special. One graduate student in her twenties recalled, "When I was young, I walked home from school with my best friend. Every day she would say, 'Let's stop at my grandma's house for a minute. I know she has a snack ready for us. I promise we won't stay long!' Little did my friend know how I loved stopping at her grandmother's house or how deeply I longed to have a grandma of my very own."

We were touched by the enthusiasm women expressed when they talked about their grandmothers. While a few told of grandparents who had been a negative influence in their lives, by far the majority spoke glowingly of the warmth, love, acceptance they had received from their grandparents.

We found that men wanted to talk about their grandmothers, too, and occasionally a man would even respond to our survey. One was a minister of a large church who said, "I am in the ministry today because of my grandmother. She used to whisper in my ear that when I grew up I was going to have a great influence on other people's lives because I was going to be a preacher. When I got into my teen years, I used to laugh at her and say, 'Oh, Grandma, don't tell me that. I'm old enough to decide for myself what I want to do.' Yet here I am. And when I stand in my pulpit, I can still hear Grandma whispering encouragement in my ear."

What can grandmothers do? They can believe in their grandchildren and encourage them to be the best they can be. Grandmothers can model love in a very special way. A granddaughter who is now the mother of three little ones said, "My grandma taught me how to love my own children. She always made time for me. When I walked into her house, no matter what she was doing, she would drop it and say, 'Let's sit down and have a cup of tea.' Then she would ask me all about my week at school and listen carefully to everything I had to say. She was always on my side. It is because of her that I am the kind of parent I am today."

One woman said, "My little old grandma always took up for me. My father was an alcoholic and my mother was always preoccupied with dealing with his drinking and violent behavior. Many nights as I lay terrified in my bed, my face turned to the wall as I tried desperately not to hear what was going on in the next room, I would think about Grandma praying for me. I gained great strength from that. And I knew that Grandma, even though she was battling severe illness herself, would soon invite me over for a weekend, and when I got to her house she would just love me to death. She would tell me I was a very special person and that whatever was going on with Dad, it had nothing to do with who I was. If I am emotionally healthy today—and I truly believe I am—I give Grandma all the credit. I hate to think what I'd be like if it weren't for her!"

## Grandmothering Joys

Any barriers that might keep us from being special grandmothers can be hurdled, even on grandmother legs. And it's worth hurdling, for on the other side of the barriers lies grandmother joy. We agree with Rolaine Hochstein, who said in her article in *Parents* magazine (June 1992), "The best thing about the empty nest is that there's room in it for grandchildren."

In this first part of *The Grandmother Book,* we will be looking at the joys of grandmothering in relation to the expectations placed on us, as well as the pressures and concerns we encounter in this new phase of our lives.

Many of the joys of grandmothering come from the gifts we have to share with our grandchildren (and we do have many to offer). We will see how these gifts are influenced by our own styles of grandmothering. Each style brings with it elements that make it easier for us to share certain gifts, as well as elements that present challenges. Neither of us have struggled with the kind of problems Jan witnessed between Jenny and her grandparents. But we know we have had problems fulfilling our grandmothering roles. Rather than being uninvolved in our grandchildren's lives, we both tend to be too involved, although in different ways. That's why the different styles of grandparenting we will explore in Chapters 5 and 6 are so important. Knowing your style of grandmothering will allow you to maximize your strengths and be on your guard against tendencies that can cause problems. Knowing your strengths can help you feel comfortable in being more involved and in helping you know your limits.

Can grandmas make a difference in the lives of their grandchildren? Absolutely! But it takes energy and love—and a good bit of know-how certainly doesn't hurt. Making a positive difference will be the theme of the chapters to come. But first, let's look at that new name that has become our own: Grandma.

## Chapter 2

# A New Name: I Think
# He Said "Grandma!"

*T*he animated chatter died down as the women we had invited to our grandmothers group settled into their seats. A glance at the women assembled proved that grandmas do indeed come in all shapes and sizes and colors, and in many ages as well. Some wore floral housedresses, some sported fancy sweat suits decorated with gold and rhinestones, and more than a few arrived in business suits. Some were relaxed, happily settling in for an afternoon of fun and sharing, while others were saying, "I can't stay very long. I have to get back to the office."

Some of the women came with their lunches in brown paper bags. Others brought beautiful baskets with enough food to share with those who might have forgotten to bring something to eat. A few planned a very special luncheon; they brought tablecloths and lovely table settings—one even carried crystal goblets. Some brought along things they had made to show the others—aprons and quilts and handmade dolls. Others had only their questions and ideas and experiences to share.

One thing everyone brought was pictures. And what

pictures they were! There were snapshots of children of all ages and nationalities. There were photographs of babies wrapped in their first blankets, proudly being displayed by brand-new moms and dads. There were graduation pictures, portraits of families, even photos of family pets.

The one thing all these ladies had in common was that every one of them had someone who called her "Grandma." Besides jumping at the opportunity to proudly show off their grandchildren, these women had come together to share and compare their grandmothering joys and challenges. We had invited them because we wanted to hear their stories, perceptions, philosophies on grandmothering. We wanted to find out from these in-the-field experts what grandmas are really facing as they try to fit into this special niche.

As these women were inspired and encouraged by each other and as they learned from others in the group, they inspired and encouraged and taught us. We are certain they will do the same for you as we share their ideas with you in this book.

### *A Grandmother by Any Name . . .*

Whether our grandchildren call us Grandmother or Grandma or Grans or Granny or Nana or Mammaw or Gamaw or something else, the name denotes a very special position in life. When a grandchild is born, so is a grandmother. One wise grandmother observed, "I don't guess it takes much to *become* a grandma. All you have to do is survive until your child has a child. It's a lot harder to *be* a grandma. It's tough to sit by and let your own child take care of that new baby!"

Whatever our grandchildren call us, we quickly find an exciting new meaning to the name. One grandma told us when she calls her granddaughter's house, her three-year-old granddaughter sometimes answers with, "What's up, Frams?" How's that for a welcoming greeting?

Another grandma said that from the minute her grandson could say his first words, he called her "Sweetie." When this grandma visited, the little one would stand up in his crib early every morning and call out at the top of his voice, "Sweeeetie! Sweeeetie!" That was years ago, but even today when this grandma calls her grandson's house, whoever answers the telephone calls out to the family, "Sweetie is on the phone!"

Another grandmother kiddingly told the group that she was teaching her grandchildren to call her "G. G." What does G. G. stand for? Why, "Gorgeous Grandmother," of course!

### So, Grandma, How Does It Feel?

Becoming a grandmother is an experience like no other. It elicits deep and powerful feelings in almost every one of us. Although we often smile at the silliness we see coming from even the most proper, straight-laced grandmothers, we still share their joy. One sent us a card expressing it this way: "Your children are your investment. Your grandchildren are your dividends."

As we talked to the women in our grandma meeting, and as we read the stories many others wrote in response to our questionnaire, an exciting picture of grandmotherhood began to emerge. What enthusiasm! What joy! What dedication! And what determination to be the very best grandmother possible. "Second chances in life are rare," one grandmother told us. "Being a grandparent is the very precious gift of a second chance."

Another lady added, "Being a grandparent is almost like

being a mother again, only better. When my own children were young, I was ill with polio. That cheated all of us out of so much of our time together. But this time around, I have lots of time. It's wonderful!"

Another grandma observed, "Grandchildren help you look backward and forward." Isn't it wonderful when we catch glimpses of ourselves in our grandchildren? "When I see my granddaughter toss the dish towel over her shoulder as she works in the kitchen, just like I do, I feel a real sense of satisfaction," the small, gray-haired woman shared.

A tall, salt-and-pepper-haired grandmother agreed, but added, "When I see so much of myself in my granddaughter, it scares me. At times I can tell what she is thinking, and I can even predict what she will do or say. But at the same time, I love it. It's like getting a chance to live all over again."

Others want to make up for the past that never was. "I want to try to be the kind of grandmother I didn't have," said one young grandma. "My greatest joy comes when I realize my grandchildren really want to be with me. When I call over to their house and ask if they can come for a visit, I hear them in the background shouting, 'Yeah, yeah, we are going to Grandma's house!' I can't tell you what that means to me."

How does it feel to be a grandmother? According to the ones we talked to it feels great! Speaking for many, one grandmother said, "My grandchildren are truly the joy of my life. I guess I sound like any proud grandma, but these grandchildren of mine are the greatest kids in the world! I once saw a little girl wearing a T-shirt that read, 'I am the cutest, smartest child in the world.' Down below that it said, 'Just ask my grandma!' That's how I feel about my grandkids. The neatest thing of all is that they love me right back and tell me I am the greatest grandma in the world. I just can't describe the feeling that gives me."

One grandma, Peggy Coholan, wrote this poem in response to our questionnaire:

### A Grandmother's Reflection

The house is quiet now.
No cautious slapping of small hard-soled shoes
Hurrying to nowhere across the wooden floors.
Just one lonely Cheerio beneath a chair,
A single sentinel reminding her he'd been
    there.
She no longer feels his small hand upon her
    knee,
Nor sees his eager eyes trying to communicate
    his needs.
"Wa, wa."
She leans to his level and asks kindly,
"You want a drink of water, Matt?"
His head shakes like a ball on a string.
They understand each other.
She glances out the kitchen window and sees
    the tree
They climbed in the front yard.
She remembers the rough bark beneath her legs
    and thinks,
How high those branches must seem to a boy
    not yet two.
They sat on the ground in her garden that day
And moved one hole to another.
She smiles and thinks, dirt is fun.
This morning she found a perfect print on the
    glass door
Where he had bravely braced himself for one
    giant step
Onto the terrace, alone.

It wasn't the only print he'd left.
He'd left his print on her heart as well.

Peggy Coholan
*Dedicated to Matthew Adair Grimshaw*

How does it feel to be a grandmother? It feels like loving deeply and being deeply loved. It feels like great hope, like getting a new lease on life, like wonderful joy and healthy pride. It feels like nothing else ever can.

## What Do Grandchildren Say?

What do you think of when you hear the word *grandma?* "What do you remember about your own grandmother?" we asked the women at our grandmothers group.

One of the virtues women attributed to their grandmothers again and again was unconditional love. What a wonderful gift for a grandmother to give to her grandchild! Said one woman, "At a critical time in my life, when I needed a safe environment to rebuild and heal, Grandma and Grandpa opened their hearts and home to me. I am so thankful for that. I want to be the same kind of grandparent for my grandchildren."

Said another, "My grandma's house was a place where I could have fun and no one yelled at me. What I got from her were hugs, kisses, gifts, and outings to special places. Grandma was always there for me, and she still is. She gave me the only true acceptance I ever had as a child."

Are you having trouble remembering your grandmother? Sometimes the memories are so far back in our minds it's hard to pull them up. "The other day I was wondering how come I so enjoyed being out in the garden," Jan's daughter-in-law Terri recalled. "There's just something about having my hands in the dirt that gives me a wonderfully warm, satisfied feeling deep inside. Then all of a sudden it struck me. Digging in the dirt was one of my favorite things Grandma let me do with her. I don't think I had ever actually thought of it before. Those memories must be lying there just below the surface of my thoughts, feeding me feelings as warm and tender as a gentle hug!"

A grandchild wrote a special story for us about her grandmother. In the envelope she enclosed a crayon-drawn picture with a caption that read, "This was my grandma. Wasn't she beautiful!"

## Treasure from Grandma

If you were lucky enough to know one or both of your grandmothers, you may well have special treasures from her. Oh, we don't mean money or jewelry or antique furniture, although some of you may have that as well. The treasure we're thinking of is far more precious, and its value is reserved just for you. Pam McComb-Podmostko wrote of such a treasure as she answered our survey.

Pam's grandmother's most prized possession was a five-by-seven portrait of Grandpa that she kept in a frame on her dresser for more than fifty years. Each time Grandma walked past her dresser she motioned her hand as if to wave, and she would say "hi" to "my Bob." Grandma wouldn't have given that photo up for a million dollars.

Since Pam lived in another state, she wasn't able to visit her grandmother very often, but every time she did, Grandma gave her a box of "treasures" to open when she got home. Although the treasures weren't worth much in dollars and cents, they were always precious to Pam, for in them she saw Grandma sharing something of herself.

After an especially enjoyable visit when Pam and Grandma worked together on an oral family history, Grandma said good-bye and, as usual, handed Pam a box of treasures to open when she got home. There were the usual things—little dishes, old family letters, and the like. But when Pam got to the bottom of the box, she noticed something very carefully wrapped in tissue paper and tied with a ribbon. Gently she untied it to find Grandma's greatest treasure in all the world—the portrait of Grandpa that had stood for all those years on Grandma's dresser.

"I was proud and honored that Grandma would give her most prized possession to me," Pam wrote. "Then suddenly I felt terribly afraid. There could only be one reason she parted with it. She must have known her time on this earth was growing short."

A few months later, Pam's grandmother had a stroke. Although Pam had been told it wouldn't be worth the expense of the airplane trip to visit her comatose grandmother, she packed her bag and went anyway. Carefully Pam tucked "Grandma's Bob" in her suitcase. She knew if anything would get a response, it would be that picture.

Pam was not prepared for the woman she found on the bed in her grandma's hospital room. She took Grandma's thin hand, rubbed it and talked to her. No response. Pam begged Grandma to open her eyes and look at what she had brought. No response.

Pam didn't give up. Again and again and again she tried to rouse Grandma. Three days later, Pam saw Grandma struggle to open her eyes. "It was only momentarily but I showed her the photo of her Bob," Pam said. "She looked at it, then her eyes met mine. Our hearts touched and once again her eyes closed. A single tear rolled down her cheek."

Pam's grandmother never opened her eyes again. She died quietly two months later.

Is Pam McComb-Podmostko a wealthy lady? You bet she is! Her grandmother left her a priceless treasure of shared love.

What are you doing to put away a treasure for your grandchildren? Are you storing away memories of unconditional love, understanding, and acceptance? Are you making consistent investments of time and attention with your grandchildren? Are you using your gifts to individually build up each one of them?

Give yourself permission to enjoy your new name and your new role in life. Rejoice in who you are, and take joy in each of your grandchildren too. You say you want to boast and brag on them? Great! Do it! Grandparents are expected to see their grandchildren as the most perfect, the most beautiful, the smartest, most talented children in the world. So go ahead and brag. Pull out the pictures. Tell the cute stories and repeat the clever sayings. It's your right as a grandma.

As one of the ladies in our grandmothers group said so eloquently, "We grammies are special people. We love, we care, we are there."

Yes, we are, and yes, we do!

# Chapter 3

◉

# *A New Role: What's Expected of Me Now?*

While traveling in the Northwest in late summer, Jan and her husband, Dave, drove down a little dead-end street toward a small park. As they pulled onto the sandy berm at the side of the road, they came upon an interesting twosome: a woman who looked to be in her sixties, clad in khaki walking shorts, a safari jacket, and wide-brimmed straw hat, and a little fellow of about ten in shorts, striped T-shirt, and a well-worn baseball cap.

The striking thing about these two was the young boy's obvious fascination with what the lady was showing him. He stood behind her, peering intently over her shoulder and through the magnifying glass she held over a small leaf on the bush before them. They called each other "Grandma" and "Buddy" as they exclaimed about what they saw. Grandma, who was doing most of the talking, was animated as she pointed out the features of the leaf.

"See the difference here?" she asked.

"Oh, wow!" Buddy replied with the same enthusiasm he showed for everything Grandma showed him.

Obviously Grandma enjoyed studying plants and their

foliage, and she was sharing this love with her grandson. As for Buddy, he was taking in far more than his grandmother's excitement about nature. What he was getting would last him a lifetime: love and attention from someone very special to him—the kind that can make a real difference in how he experiences life, the kind that can give him a foundation on which to build the confidence he will need to get through the tough experiences of life.

What is your grandmothering role in the lives of your grandchildren? How has that role changed since the days of your own grandmother?

## Grandparents, Historically Speaking

Before the 1960s, very little was written about the grandparenting role. In their book *The New American Grandparent* Andrew J. Cherlin and Frank F. Furstenberg, Jr., say grandparents were sometimes mentioned with a mere comment on what was called the "grandparent syndrome," a situation in which it was thought the developing child might well be harmed by a meddling third-generation adult. In the 1940s and 1950s, a great deal of research time was spent on marriage, with only a secondary emphasis on the parent-child relationship. Grandparenting issues, not considered important enough to warrant much effort, were far down the list.

Many of us who were born in the 1920s and 1930s remember our grandparents as quiet influences in our lives. One woman recalled, "My own grandma was quiet, but we all knew who was in charge. We never contradicted her, not even when she was wrong. I never knew her as a friend."

Another said, "My grandma was to be respected above

all else. She was so respected I would never have thought of asking her to get down and play with us, as I do with my grandchildren. I can't imagine her even thinking about marching around the house, leading a children's parade with a silly hat on her head as I do, now that I'm a grandma. That would have been far too unladylike for her. Maybe that's why I don't feel I ever got close to her. Things were really rough for me growing up, and as I look back I try to imagine what it would have been like if I could have had a relationship with my grandmother that was safe and close."

One adult grandchild told us, "I was afraid of my grandmother. She never did anything to me, but her words and looks seemed to be so strict. She lived with us for awhile, and I can remember her sitting at the same spot at the table for those years, with me seated right next to her. I had to always be on guard, for if I didn't eat properly or if I made some mistake in etiquette, she would give my dad a certain look and he would tell me to leave the table."

Why the difference? In earlier times, the role of a grandmother was seen differently. Few doubted that their grandmothers loved them or that Grandma would be there when the chips were down, but often a grandmother's emotional involvement in the life of her grandchild was minimal. Few grandmothers were thought of as companions or pals or even friends.

Of course, there were exceptions, as we learned in the previous chapters. But positive grandmother roles were generally limited to modeling strength and ability and the spiritual fortitude to hang in there when times were tough.

By the sixties, things began to change. With divorce rates skyrocketing, sociologists and psychologists began to look more closely at the American family. What they saw was that grandparents had become more important. But as they became more important, they were thrust into roles they hadn't known before. Now grandmas and grandpas were being called upon to enrich the lives of grandchildren who were stressed out by changes in their own families and by the pressures of the rapidly changing world.

In the seventies, grandparents were portrayed in an even greater role. In such television programs as "The Waltons," we saw grandparents as an integral part of the extended family. Instead of distant role models, they were actually a part of the nurturing process in the life of a child. Grandparents liked what they saw. They knew they had a lot to offer, and they were all for close-up involvement.

As grandparents offered more of themselves, they began to ask for more as well. They wanted to be able to see their grandchildren and to have a relationship with them, even if there were problems in the family. And so in the late seventies and early eighties, great numbers of grandparents began to fight for their rights. Even though judges were reluctant to interfere in the parenting process, most ruled that grandparents really do have a right to be with their grandchildren. (We'll discuss grandparents' rights more in Chapter 17.)

Aren't you glad you're a grandmother today? We are a generation of grandparents more able and better equipped to fulfill the newly defined role of grandparenting. We can do it better than ever!

## The Balancing Act

We grandmas of today are presented with an intricate balancing act. Being busy ladies, we sometimes have trouble keeping our priorities straight. It's hard to pull away from our hectic lifestyles and concentrate on building a relationship with our grandchildren. We expound the joys of grandmotherhood, yet we sometimes feel discouraged, taken advantage of, and disappointed.

Our newly found freedom to be more involved and our understanding of how important we are in the lives of our grandchildren don't prevent us from sometimes feeling unappreciated and unwanted by our own children. We want to give what we can to our grandchildren, but we also want to keep their parents happy. One grandmother who well knows this dilemma wrote, "I would gladly spend more time with my grandchildren, but my daughter-in-law doesn't seem to want me around. It almost feels like I'm in competition with her for her children's love. I would never have it that way, so I find it best to keep myself too busy to dwell on the hurt I feel."

Perhaps you thought you knew what the grandmother's role was, but now you're discovering a lot of disturbing unknowns. We certainly can relate to that. Our well-known penchant for spoiling our grandchildren aside, most of us really want to know where the boundaries lie. What are we responsible for and what is none of our business? We know what it is to be a child, a friend, a wife, and a parent. We have experience in all those roles. But what does it mean to be a grandma?

Since it is the relationship with our grandchildren's parents that often presents us with the greatest problems, let's look first at that relationship.

## *Our Role in the Lives of Our Own Children*

Most grandmothers who spoke of the negative aspects of grandparenting observed—only half kiddingly—that they would know exactly how to fill their role as grandma if their own kids (the parents) didn't get in the way.

The problem is that too many of us loving, well-meaning grandmas tend to "take over." We don't mean to. It's just that something triggers our parenting instincts and we can't seem to help ourselves. It's hard to think of our own children as being capable of parenting without our help. One grandma kiddingly said, "No one in her right mind would ever trust her own child, who never had the sense to come in out of the rain, to raise a baby!"

Another grandma put it this way: "When we become grandmothers, our job has only begun. Now we have to supervise everything. We have to oversee the sterilization of bottles, see that diapers are changed properly, teach about temperature taking and the best position for burping, and always make sure the baby isn't too warm or too cold. Our job is very complicated!"

Our children resent us taking over, but we feel responsible to see that the job is done right. No wonder there are problems.

## The Chain Reaction

Today we hear the term "dysfunctional family" buzzing around everywhere. In their book *Creating a Safe Place,* Curt Grayson and Jan Johnson describe dysfunction as "an inability to relate to God and others because we were nurtured improperly as children." David Seamands, in his book *Healing for Damaged Emotions,* calls this a chain reaction. He wrote, "Beginning with the first sin of Adam and Eve, there was set in motion a chain reaction of imperfect parenting, through failures and ignorance and misguided actions, and worst of all, through conditional love."

As grandparents, we may find it painful to realize we are a part of that chain reaction, especially as we see our adult children repeating some of the same parenting mistakes we made with them. Looking at the matter from our different perspective, we are certain the problem could be fixed if only our sons or daughters would listen to us. (Never mind that we didn't listen when our parents tried to tell us!)

Who is right, we or our kids? Probably both—and neither. Parenting is not a perfect science. Our parenting was imperfect, and our children's will be too. That's not to say all parenting is so inadequate that it will cause disturbing behaviors in children. It's just that no matter how good the parenting, it won't be perfect.

Back when we were raising our children, our goal was to lead them into healthy, independent adulthood. Now that our grandchildren have come along, our tendency is to grab up the parenting mantle and jump back into the task, complete with instructions and corrections. It's our chance to correct all the mistakes we made the first time around.

A better, healthier role for us is that of gentle, cautious adviser.

## A Gentle, Cautious Adviser

We can be involved in the lives of our grandchildren and their parents without pushing ourselves into the position of power. Anytime we try to get power or take it away from someone else, our relationships suffer. That's why it's vital that we avoid power struggles. Most of us insist, "Oh, that's not me. If anything, I try my best not to interfere." Our intentions are good. Our motives are pure. But too often that old need for power sneaks out in subtle ways and takes over.

Some grandmothers push for power by "innocently"

asking questions such as "Do you think the baby is hungry?" "Doesn't Jeremy need a haircut even if he doesn't want it?" Those questions sound innocent enough, but underneath are strong, unspoken messages: *You aren't taking proper care of the baby,* or *You should take charge of Jeremy.* Anytime we try to get our message across indirectly, we are trying to exert power over the parent.

"I know this is how I tend to pressure my kids," Jan admitted. "I offer to help way too much. I want to take care of things for them."

The problem with over-helping is that when you say, "You go rest and let me take care of it," your adult child's reaction is often, "What? You don't think I can do anything!" Helping too much makes you feel powerful and the other person feel inadequate.

You might be asking, "How can I be exerting too much power when I'm offering to do good things?" Try asking parents. They say they are often intimidated by grandparents who offer too much and who are so terribly capable. One young mother told us, "Whenever my mother-in-law takes care of the kids, I come home to a freshly vacuumed house, whiter laundry, and a cleaner refrigerator. The kids love her. She is incredible at handling them and making it all fun. They beg to have her come over. But it bugs me so much that I seldom ask her to baby-sit."

Poor Grandma! Sometimes she just can't win!

Or can she? With a bit of insight we can have a win-win situation, but it means giving up all illusions of power, especially the subtle, hidden ones. (We'll talk more about power struggles in Chapter 12.) It is our responsibility to recognize just who the parents are, to respect the boundaries they set, and to allow them to be in charge.

A good adviser holds back her advice until she is asked

for it. She knows when to talk and when to keep quiet. She is able to squelch the impulse to jump in and fix things.

"My daughter says I interfere too much," one grandmother told us sadly. "I was so excited about her first baby. I took my daughter shopping for baby things; I dreamed and planned with her. I even took time off work to stay with her when Jeffy was born. But after a few days, it became obvious my presence wasn't appreciated. I left with angry feelings all around. I honestly don't know what I did wrong."

If this sounds at all familiar, work at understanding how you use your power. Talk the problem over with your son or daughter. Ask what happened. (Be prepared. Your child just may come back with some real gripes!) Resist the temptation to be defensive. Remember, your goal is to open communication, not close it. When you have talked it over, take the initiative and accept the responsibility for improving the situation.

If your adult child's family lives out of state, try writing a letter. Or write out your feelings for yourself, going over in your mind what caused the problem, then make a blanket apology: "I'm not sure exactly what happened, but I want you to know I didn't intend it and I am sorry."

Jan said, "Even when I've determined to keep my opinions to myself, I can't. The pull to jump in and be the adviser is too strong." On a recent trip with several families, she and her grandchildren were playing with little balloons. Everyone was having fun until Jan's son suddenly decided it was time for his daughter to go. Her little granddaughter was heartbroken because she couldn't finish the project. "It made me very unhappy," Jan recalled, "and I said things I wish I hadn't. I wish I could have stayed out of it."

It's not always easy to be gentle and noncritical. We know it's not. But it's important enough to work on it.

## Sensitive Stand-in

A very special role we grandmothers can play in the lives of our grandchildren's parents is that of stand-in. "I remember the days when I was a young parent with three active sons," Jan said. "So many times I wished Grandma was closer so I could leave one or all of the boys with her for a day. I needed a break!"

It's great when a grandmother can step in and take over when she is needed, but she needs to be sensitive and flexible enough to be able to step away when Mommy returns.

It's not easy to give up the parent role. Once a mother, always a mother.

One aware grandma told us, "After I have had little Mara for several days, I find it really hard to let go of her. I get to know all her special needs, that she has to have her little stuffed dog and blanket a certain way and that she only likes apple-grape juice. And she changes so quickly that some of her little quirks develop while her parents are away. But I have learned the hard way not to make a big deal to them about what Mara needs and all she has learned. I have to let it all go and let her parents find out for themselves. Otherwise, they seem to think I know too much. I have to play it their way and let them be in control."

Can you give up some of the joy of sharing the baby's newest trick in lieu of the deeper satisfaction of knowing you're accepted in the family? Can you be satisfied to be a stand-in rather than the one in charge? If so, you are a wise grandma indeed.

## Loving, Supportive Encourager

Our grown children need to know we are on their team. When a grandmother can brag not only about her grandchildren, but also about all the wonderful things their parents do with them, she is fulfilling the role of loving, supportive encourager. For, while we have a hard time seeing our children as adult enough to parent, we also tend to see them as too independent to need the love and affirmation we joyfully bestow on their children.

Isn't it easy to offer "constructive criticism" to our kids? Yet studies conducted among workers show that criticism is not only demoralizing, it works completely counter to what it's supposed to accomplish. However, when a boss compliments a worker for doing something well, that worker is motivated and begins to improve performance even in his or her weak areas. Criticism, even if we are convinced it is for our kids' own good, isn't going to work. The way to help them become better parents is to acknowledge and admire their efforts and successes.

Is it sometimes hard to find qualities to admire and encourage in your children's parenting style? If you look carefully enough, you will find something. If you feel it is absolutely necessary to say something negative, especially if you see your grandchild being harmed by a parent's attitude or actions, try to sit down with the parents and talk about your concerns. Even though your comments may not be taken well, it is your only real alternative. Your attempts to get your message across in less direct ways have almost no chance of being accepted. The result of indirect communication will be that you'll be kept at a distance.

It is just as important to be direct in your compliments.

Make sure your admiring statements come through loud and clear.

Gentle advice, sensitive standing-in, and supportive encouraging—these are the things that make a successful, fulfilled grandmother. Such a grandma has the freedom to be pleasantly active in the lives of her grandchildren. The entire family wants her there!

### Creating a Safe Place for Our Grandchildren

Not all of us will be called upon to provide our grand-children with physical protection and safety, but we all have a responsibility to provide for our grandchildren's emotional needs. It's hard to know what will make a real difference in the life of a child. One grandma wrote and told us of a grandma who found the perfect thing to say. On her granddaughter's wedding day she took the brand-new husband aside, put her arm around his shoulder, and whispered in his ear, "You're so lucky. I hope you know she could have had her pick of many!"

All of us need a place where we can really be ourselves—a safe place where it's okay to let down and relax, comfortable in the knowledge that we will be loved no matter what. We need to know that in one place our cause will be championed and someone will always stand up for us. Those who go through childhood without this kind of place often become adults who are lonely, who have trouble trusting others, who even push away the very people who could provide them with comfort and safety. And when they set up family systems of their own, they don't know how to create safe places for their own children.

In dysfunctional families, children can often find that place of safety and unconditional love with Grandma. For them, Grandma can make a lifetime of difference. One woman shared that when she was two years old, her five-year-old brother died suddenly. Her mother was so devastated she gave up on life and withdrew; it was all she could do to care for her six-month-old baby brother. "My grandma thought it was best if I moved in with her. She and I got each other through that terrible time." Then she paused for a minute and added, "Your asking about my grandmother opened up the floodgate. I have more wonderful memories about her than I could tell you in a year!"

Another woman in her thirties told us, "When I was four, my mother had a mental breakdown, and for the rest of her life she was in and out of psychiatric hospitals. When she was at home, I never knew what was going to happen. Many times I was left to play by myself all day while she stayed in her room sleeping. Dad was so overwhelmed trying to work and hold the family together he didn't even notice what was going on with me. It was Grandma who provided the only stability in my life."

Sometimes it's just a grandmother's attitude that lets her grandchild know a safe haven is there. "Grandma never really talked about it, but I always knew she was available to me, even when she was far away," one woman explained. "I knew I could call her any time of the day or night and she would say, 'I'm so glad you called!'"

You can create a safe place for your grandchildren through your attitude, through your words, and through your actions.

## Creating a Safe Place Through Your Attitude

Your attitude will set the tone. Want an example? Look at God's character. The following characteristics are adapted from David Seamands's book *Healing for Dam-*

*aged Emotions*. Contrast the godly characteristics of
safety in the first column with their unsafe counter-
characteristics in the second:

| Safe | Unsafe |
| --- | --- |
| Available | Too busy |
| Merciful | Unforgiving |
| Loving | Hateful |
| Caring | Unconcerned |
| Nurturing | Critical |
| Accepting | Rejecting |
| Just | Unjust |
| Fair | Unfair |
| Reliable | Untrustworthy |
| Giving | Withholding |
| Steadfast | Unpredictable |

Dysfunctional families are riddled with the characteristics on the unsafe list, but even the best of families have
some of them. In the absence of a healthy support system,
those unsafe attitudes damage a child. Consider the attitude of unfairness. A child can tolerate unfairness if he or
she knows the person or situation isn't always going to be
unfair, that his or her turn is coming. But if the child learns
life is always going to be unfair day after day, he or she
gives up hope and sinks into despair.

A grandparent can counteract negative attitudes,
whether they are real or only exist in the child's mind. She
can create a different atmosphere for the child. But remember, no parent wants his children to feel safer at
Grandma's house than at his own home. The trick is to
discover ways to counteract these negative attitudes without causing the child's parents to feel threatened. It's the
balancing act again; it takes great courage and skill.

Children are great at picking up on attitudes. Teenagers, too, are keenly tuned in to underlying messages. Are you serious about your attitudes? Look through the list of safe attitudes once more, and put a check beside each one to which you are willing to make a true commitment. Now see if you can think of specific ways to demonstrate each of those attitudes to your grandchildren.

(One warning: If there is a real and immediate danger to your grandchild, cast aside your quiet attitude and take action, no matter what the toll on your relationship with his or her parents.)

## Creating a Safe Place Through Your Words

Many times we can counteract unsafe situations by allowing our grandchildren to talk them out when they are alone with us. It's helpful to be able to talk and respond in safe language; in doing so we give respect to a child with our words. Certainly affirming words such as "You are special to me, and I love you," are musts. But the way we speak them is also important.

Look at the following responses and see if you can catch the different feelings a child may have from hearing them.

A child says, "I'm afraid to go in there. It's too dark!"
*Unsafe response:* "You're too big to be afraid of the dark!"
*Safe response:* "Lots of people are afraid of the dark. Let's talk about why they might be afraid."

A child says to his or her brother, "I hate you!"
*Unsafe response:* "You've made your brother very angry."
*Safe response:* "Your brother is very angry. I want you to talk to him and work out your problem."

A child is swinging his toy around too close to the baby.
*Unsafe response:* "Don't play close to the baby like that. You are going to hurt him."
*Safe response:* "Can you play over there? It's safer and the baby can watch you better."

A young teenager complains, "Mom says I have to get my hair cut. She just doesn't understand!"
*Unsafe response:* "You'd better obey your mom. You may not realize it now, but she is doing it for your own good."
*Safe response:* "Hair is important, isn't it? Why do you suppose she wants you to get it cut?"

A teenager says, "I'm moving out. I can't stand it at my house any more!"
*Unsafe response:* "You'd better talk to your dad about it. He's going to be very angry!"
*Safe response:* "Let's talk about it first. What's going on that makes you feel you need to do that?"

Did you notice that in each case one response is threatening and the other is nonthreatening? Did you see that the nonthreatening response gives an opportunity for discussion? Nonthreatening and open communication, that's the way to create a safe place with your words.

One grandma said, "My son won't listen to his children. He accuses, disciplines harshly, and does all the talking. He is especially hard on our grandson and belittles him constantly. Whenever I get a chance, I try to get those two kids to open up and talk to me. They are hesitant to say how things are going at home, but at least they talk to me about problems at school and their lives in general. I think my most important job is to be a friend who listens and will never betray their confidence."

Comforting phrases, messages of encouragement, interactive questions—these are wonderfully effective ways of creating a safe place for our grandchildren. While words cannot cover up our attitudes, they can confirm what our grandchildren are already picking up. If what we say matches our attitudes, our grandchildren will begin to learn to trust us. If they do not match, our grandchildren will be left with questions about our trustworthiness.

Just as our words can affirm, so can they wound. An older lady told us this story: "I was sitting at a table in a restaurant next to a grandmother and her little grandson, Jeremy. Throughout lunch she called the boy 'stupid' and 'lazy.' She tried to control him with threats such as, 'If you don't eat this, I may just leave you here!' It was all I could do to keep from going over and punching that woman!"

Fortunately, most of us are wiser and more in control than little Jeremy's grandmother. Yet many of us catch ourselves thoughtlessly tossing verbal hurts at our grandchildren. When we allow our anger and frustration to take over, it's awfully easy to say things we really hadn't intended to say.

Our own unresolved issues are another factor in the way we work out our relationships. The words that spring from our mouths often represent more than just our response to what is happening right now. Something deeper within us, something in our past that has never been dealt with, may be the real issue. The saddest thing about unresolved issues is that they tend to pop out and injure those we love the most. We'll look at this more in Chapter 4.

In his book *The Power of a Parent's Words,* Norm Wright states, "But if we are not careful, our communication can damage them. We can make them feel worthless—or we can learn to use communication constructively and help our children think as highly of themselves as God does." It's the same with us grandmothers. Let's resolve to use our words to build up and affirm our precious grandchildren.

## Creating a Safe Place Through Your Touch

One adult grandchild said, "My grandma always smelled of garlic. How I loved that smell! When Grandma hugged me, I just knew everything was going to be all right. All the way to her house, my brother and I would say we weren't going to let her make us sit on her lap again, but when we got there, she gave us big hugs and we'd sit on her lap while she talked to us about school and things. Grandma loved us so much!"

Another said, "Even when I grew into adulthood, Granny kept right on kissing my every little hurt and making a big deal about any little scratch I'd get. To this day, I remember her being so gentle and sympathetic. When my own kids come to me with their hurts, I sometimes start to say, 'Oh, don't be such a baby.' But then I remember how Granny comforted me, and how very safe I felt around her. From Granny I learned to see that what's important to my child needs to be important to me. She demonstrated her love for me by her gentle actions."

Touch has a unique bonding effect on humans. After World War II, researchers in England were concerned about the very high death rate in the orphanages. In one orphanage, however, the death rate was about the same as in the general infant population. The only difference researchers could find there was a nurse named Anna. As she went about her daily duties, Anna carried one baby after another along with her. She cuddled and soothed the tiny bodies as each in turn bounced along with her. It was Anna's touch, the researchers concluded, that gave her tiny charges the will to live. Gentle, loving touching can literally make the difference between life and death.

Some grandmothers find it difficult to hold and hug their grandchildren because they were not held and hugged when they were growing up. As awkward as it may feel, Grandma, it is important to touch and hug and kiss and hold your grandchildren.

"Physical touching was not a part of our family, so hugging and holding are difficult for me," one grandmother told us. "But I am determined that pattern will change. The great thing is, as I do it, it becomes easier. Maybe if I keep practicing with my grandchildren, I'll someday be able to hug my own children."

More power to that grandmother!

Creating a safe place for our grandchildren can involve many things. It includes the many gifts of grandmothering we will cover in Part 2 of *The Grandmother Book*. But in all of these things, our overriding attitude, our words, and our touch must tell our grandchildren, *This is a safe place for you. You are welcome here!*

## Chapter 4

&#10086;

# A New Stage in Life: Where Did the Time Go?

*W*here are your glasses? You won't be able to read the menu," a small, white-haired woman seated at a restaurant booth asked her elderly husband in a scolding voice. "You'll be bothering the waitress with your silly questions all evening." When her husband commented that the chicken looked good, she said, "You know you shouldn't order the chicken. You're never satisfied with it. Honestly, you're getting so dense. Do I have to remember everything for you?"

"Why don't you mind your own business?" her husband snapped. "You don't know everything! I'm hungry for chicken and I'm going to order chicken, no matter what you say. I'll make my own decisions!"

Jan and Dave, sitting in the booth next to the couple, looked at each other. "We had often discussed what old age was going to bring to us," Jan explained. "Would it eventually be like this, squabbling and bossing and nipping at each other's throats? We prayed not."

The problem is the tendency for any negative traits we have in our earlier years to grow and intensify with age.

Reminding becomes nagging. Slight stubbornness becomes dig-in-your-heels bullheadedness.

Years ago, speaker and author Betty Coble said her goal in life was to become a "sweet little old lady."

"I've never forgotten that," Jan said. "Although it caught my attention at the time, it never had the meaning it does today."

As we get older we begin to wonder, *Will I be a sweet little old lady, or will I be a bitter old woman?* That's a critical question for grandmothers to consider. We need to assume some control over where we are heading as we age. Betty Coble's point was a good one: We need to prepare for our old age by heading off attitudes and habits that can later cause us to sink into bitterness and despair.

Besides being a time of preparation, middle-age-plus is a time of finding a balance between caring for others and wanting to be cared for ourselves. This stage may involve more intensive responsibility and caregiving than any other stage of life.

You might wonder what could be more intensive than the time and responsibility it takes to care for babies and young children. Sure those years are a challenge, but the middle and later years can require even more of us. For many women, these later years mean assuming the responsibility for elderly parents. For others it means involvement with adult children who left the nest but have come back, often toting their problems and children with them. For some it means taking on the full-time parenting of grandchildren. Add to these the responsibilities of retirement, financial troubles, an ailing spouse or even his death, and you'll see the stresses that can pile up on women at this stage.

And when does all this hit us? At the very time we are having to admit we can no longer do all we used to do, when we are facing an abrupt end to our childbearing years, when the mirror convinces us we are becoming less and less attractive every week. And for many, the realization that long-held dreams will forever go unfulfilled brings a loss that shakes their very reason for living. To add the role of grandmothering on top of all this may be the final straw.

Or could it be the salvation instead?

## *The Adulthood Task*

### Generativity and Integrity

Human-development psychologist Erik Erikson calls the period of adulthood, or middle age, the crisis of "generativity," and describes it as the age span of approximately thirty-five to sixty-five. Those of you who fit into the earlier half of this age category are probably groaning at being called "middle-aged." Those of us in the latter half are relieved we're still in the group at all. Today there are many more middle-aged grandparents than there used to be. Because of the increase in life span, there are also more grandparents over age sixty-five, the stage Erikson refers to as "old age." (If you're there, don't be offended. That's just one person's title!)

In middle age, with all its transitions and adjustments, many of us begin to ask, "Was my life worth it? Did I do anything significant at all? Is it too late for me now?"

Erikson sees middle-aged persons as having two options: Either we will tend toward *generativity* or toward *stagnation*. When we evaluate our own lives, we may not be pleased with what we find. To stagnate is our greatest fear, yet it is the option many of us subtly take. What happens is we give up hope and become even more stagnated until we finally quit trying to make changes at all. Our tendency then is to focus on our regrets about our past.

Certainly there is nothing wrong with taking a personal inventory of what we have done with our lives. Doing so helps us see that things can be done differently. But dwelling on questions about our worth and the value of our lives often turns our focus to our regrets rather than to the opportunities that still lie ahead. Because regrets keep us turned inward and focused on what we have not done, they cannot pull us out of our stagnation. Inevitable questions about life may precipitate a crisis as we look at the little time we have left in which to do something "meaningful." When we are stuck in a position of stagnation, our emphasis will be on the "do" when we ask ourselves the question, "What can I do that will be worth anything?"

On the other hand, Erikson defines generativity as concern for what is going to happen *after* us. It is caring for the things outside ourselves. When we speak of generativity, we mean we have something to pass on. A better question than "What have I done with my life?" might be "What can I pass on to those who come after me?" Notice how this question implies a sense of hope. It infers that we have something to leave to others, that we have hope there will even be another generation, that others will take up where we have left off. Here the emphasis is on "give": "What can I give at this stage of life?"

Matthew Linn, Sheila Fabricant, and Dennis Linn, in their book *Healing the Eight Stages of Life,* speak of the positive option of generativity as saying yes to the future. They describe it as "care for others beyond one's family, for future generations and for the kind of world in which these generations will live." We have created new life—our

own children—and now we are passing it on to our grandchildren and through them to many generations to come.
This is what generativity is about.

We grandmothers have many important choices before
us. Erickson describes the next stage as one which also has
two paths: Will we choose the path of *integrity* or the path
to *despair?* Despair. What a terrible sounding word. It sig-
nifies the ultimate in hopelessness. It assumes a total giving up on life. Linn, Fabricant, and Linn describe despair
as an inability to face the diminishments old age brings
and ultimately an inability to face one's own death. Integrity, on the other hand, brings an acceptance of these diminishments and wisdom in looking at one's own death.

With integrity, one can find the gift contained in the
ending of this life and the beginning of the life to come.

A friend of ours, who has taken on the task of caring for
elderly people in her home, loves to talk about George, a
client in his late eighties. Our friend says he is the most
"alive" person she knows. George has a passion for travel,
and over the years he has saved money in order to be able
to indulge in that passion. Interestingly enough, George
spends most of his time planning his next trip, which is
often to visit missionaries working in other countries. He
says he goes there to "encourage them." And he probably
does. He is so enthusiastic about life, so ready to share his
close relationship with God, so open in his dealing with
life and death, that it can't help but be contagious.

George knows all about living with integrity.

At a recent meeting of our women's Bible study, someone handed us a "grandmother" article. It was the story of
ninety-eight-year-old Bessie Moore. Bessie keeps busy
writing letters. Last spring, a schoolteacher told her third-
grade class about Bessie, and all twenty-eight students de-

cided to write to her. Two weeks later, every single child received a personal, handwritten answer. To one student Bessie wrote, "I am a happy lady so my life is good. I will see if I can find a picture to send, but it won't be beautiful. OK?"

Bessie lives with integrity.

How about you? Are you opting for integrity or despair?

Integrity asks, "What do I need to do with the rest of my life?" There is a big difference between this question and asking, "What have I failed to do?" The latter dwells on regrets over the past, while the former poses a positive question about the future. The latter opts for despair, while the former opts for integrity.

As we reach the latter stage of life, despair has such a strong pull that many cannot release themselves from its grasp. As physical and mental incapacities progress, so does the pull down into despair. Integrity, on the other hand, allows a sense of knowing that because life is drawing to an end, each moment counts. It is this embracing of life in the later years that counteracts despair.

When it comes to the struggle against the stagnation of middle age and the despair of old age, grandmothers are exceedingly vulnerable. The grandmas we interviewed said they hadn't thought of describing it in those exact terms, but they agreed they were certainly fighting *something*. When asked to describe what they were feeling, they kept coming up with the words *depression* and *tiredness* and described feelings of worthlessness.

## Grandmother Depression

Stagnation and despair could be called the precursors to depression. Many grandmothers told us they didn't want to admit to their families that they were feeling depressed. They were afraid it meant they would have to be hospitalized; older grandmas thought it might mean being put into a nursing home. Certainly some people suffering from depression do need to be treated in an inpatient setting. But the fact is that most of us feel depressed part of the time, and many experience deep depression at some time in their lives. It's nothing to be ashamed of.

Some of us aren't even sure what it is we are depressed about. Others say, "Oh, I know exactly what I'm depressed about. My life is in shambles, my kids have ruined their lives, and because of them my grandchildren are suffering terribly."

Whether or not we know the reason for it, depression is a widespread problem for grandmothers. In fact, it is our biggest mental-health problem today. In her book *Unfinished Business,* Maggie Scarf showed that up to six times as many women as men suffer from depression. And these figures only consider people who have sought professional help for it. Many don't.

## Is It Hormones?

The role hormones play in depression is the subject of a great deal of debate. Many professionals hold that there is indeed a specific physiological and biological reason why women in their menopausal years tend to experience a certain type of depressive disorder. Others insist that, no, the depression experienced by women at this stage of their lives comes because they are psychologically "stuck" in certain areas and simply cannot accept and adjust to the normal changes. Still others suggest the depression comes from a woman's more sensitive makeup that leaves her more vulnerable and less able to deal with the unresolved issues in her past and the changes and losses of her present relationships.

So who's right? No one can say for sure. Most likely it's a combination of all three. Certainly our bodies do experience major hormonal changes that can affect us in various ways. Without a doubt, the effects of unresolved psychological tasks do catch up with us. And, yes, the relationship changes we experience can be profound indeed—our children are grown with families and lives of their own, our parents are dependent on us or no longer living, we are seeing friends, or perhaps even our own spouses, die.

Whatever its cause, depression can make us miserable. It can be the source of our feelings of extreme tiredness and rob us of the most rewarding aspects of our lives, including our ability to be the effective grandmothers we want to be. So the important question becomes, "What can I do about it?" Two issues we often overlook when looking for answers are the physical and our own childhood and how it may be presently affecting us.

## Address the Physical

The place to start is with your physical self. We know, we know. *Menopause* is a word most of us would like to wipe from our vocabularies. We don't want to discuss it, we don't want to consider it, and most of all we don't want to experience it. In this day of enlightenment we talk freely about our AIDS-related fears, the word *abortion* is heard nearly every day, we join groups to talk about our painful childhoods, we even share with others about our addictions. But menopause? Few of us sit around with a friend or a group of other women and discuss this. Gail Sheehy talks about this in her recent book *The Silent Passage,* suggesting that menopause may be the last taboo. Even though forty-three million American women have experienced or are experiencing it, we still don't know how to deal with it.

According to Sheehy, this passage we all experience is seldom accomplished easily. Society doesn't offer us much help. We get conflicting medical advice and very little sympathy from our families. All this makes for a very lonely experience.

One grandmother shared this: "I have never told anyone, not even my best friend, how much trouble I am having going through 'the change.' My husband thinks I am exaggerating when I complain about being so warm, and he gets impatient with me for throwing off the covers many times every night. So I try to do it quietly, and often I just get up and go downstairs and read until I think I can go back to sleep. I am absolutely worn out by the time morning comes. Not even my doctor understands. He tells me it is too early for me to be experiencing hormonal changes and that we'll talk about it at my next checkup. That's not until next year! Why can't I go through this easily like other women? No one else seems to have all this trouble."

A sad letter indeed—not because of the woman's hot flashes, but because of the feeling of isolation she is feeling. If you see yourself in this letter, we would like to suggest several things.

**1. Get a second opinion.** Not all doctors are great at handling all areas of medicine. Many doctors out there recognize the problem and are able to help you understand and adjust to any discomforts. If you are not satisfied with what you are hearing from your doctor, get a second opinion.

**2. Talk to your friends.** There's nothing shameful about the subject. This is the way God made us women. At the very least you will find you are not alone. At best you will discover new answers and ways to cope with the discomforts.

**3. Ask your doctor to talk to your family.** Menopause is a very real condition. You deserve to have the understanding of those you live with and love.

## Consider Your Childhood Issues

One grandmother asked, "More than anything, I want to help my grandchild. But how can I? I grew up in a dysfunctional family and it's painfully clear that I carried the junk right along to my own children. How can I possibly make things different for my grandchildren?"

It's not going to be easy. But it's not impossible, either. To make a difference, we grandmas have to be actively involved with our grandchildren. We have to plunge into the game; it's not enough to stand on the sidelines and coach. We must become part of a process that begins with a very important step: dealing with our own issues. When we try to change things for our grandchildren without having first dealt with ourselves, we will simply reinforce the generational patterns of dysfunction. Yes, even when we mean well. Even when we try terribly hard.

What do we mean when we say "deal with our own issues"? Just that we are to first identify what affected us when we were growing up; then we try to understand it. To help accomplish this, ask yourself such questions as the following. (We find it extremely helpful in this kind of exercise to write out our responses.)

What do you wish your parents had done differently when you were a child?

_____

_____

_____

How do you remember feeling about these things when you were a child?

_____

_____

_____

What do you wish you could have experienced with your grandparents?

_____

_____

_____

When you think about raising your own children, what do you wish could have been different?

_____

_____

_____

Look back over your answers. Do you see any common themes?

_____

_____

_____

What are some of the inadequacies you feel when you compare yourself with other grandmothers?

_____

_____

_____

Could your feelings of inadequacy be related to your own experiences growing up?

_____

_____

_____

If so, in what ways?

_____

_____

_____

If you feel anger or sadness as you answer these questions or want to explore further the relationship with your own parents, you might want to refer to the book *Forgiving Our Parents, Forgiving Ourselves* by Jan's husband, Dr. David Stoop, and co-author Dr. James Masteller. Working through the answers to questions such as these will give you a basis for making a difference in the lives of your grandchildren. For it is when we understand our own past that we can begin to face with confidence and begin to understand the vulnerable spots in our grandchildren. Only then are we prepared to "stand in the gap" for them.

## *Grandchildren Give Us a Reason to Live*

After an especially fun time with her little granddaughter Michelle, Jan was driving her home. Suddenly Michelle asked, "How old are you, Grandma?"

"Fifty-three," Jan said. Then she added, "That's pretty old, isn't it?"

Michelle thought for a minute, then asked, "How old are people when they die?"

"Well," Jan said, "people die at all different ages, but some people live to be eighty or ninety years old."

"I wish your egg had come down at the same time as mine," Michelle said. "Don't you?"

"Egg?" Jan asked. "What do you mean, Michelle?"

"You know, Grandma," Michelle said, "when God decides to go over to the pile of eggs He has up in heaven and chooses which one will be born. I just wish He had chosen yours and mine to come down at the same time. Then we could be sisters. Maybe even twins!"

"Yes," Jan said. "That would be nice. But then I couldn't be your grandma, and you couldn't be my granddaughter."

"But we could play together and go to school together," Michelle said.

"Oh, that would be fun," Jan agreed.

A long silence filled the car. Then Michelle reached over and touched Jan's hand. In a soft voice she said, "Grandma, I don't want you to die!"

Having our grandchildren in our lives may not solve all our problems, but their need and desire for our love certainly gives us a reason to live. As we grow older, it is important that we know there is someone who truly cares whether we live or die. We all need such a person in our lives, and often it is a grandchild who fills that longing.

Grandchildren allow us to pass life along and to take

heart in what will happen after we are gone. They are the part of us that will live on through generations to come. Grandchildren help us live with integrity as they bring out in us the issues we have not yet resolved. They help us look at our lives in a new and creative way. They keep us from despair and are a wonderful antidote to depression. Grandchildren give a purpose and a meaning to a grandmother's life like little else can.

"There is a time for everything, / and a season for every activity under heaven," the preacher wrote in the book of Ecclesiastes (3:1, NIV).

It was God Himself who ordained our seasons: first a season as a child, then as a parent, and now as a grandmother. What a wonderful plan! If we can welcome this stage and hear the little voices cheering us on, how blessed we are!

# Part 2

## The Styles of Grandmothering

# Chapter 5

∾

# *If I Can't Do It All, Am I Still Okay?*

*I*n a recent "Dennis the Menace" cartoon, Dennis, sitting on his grandfather's lap, looks up and says, "It's not easy being a kid today. How is it being a grandpa?"

Well, we can tell you about being grandmas, Dennis, and that's not easy, either.

Our dear friend Arvella Schuller, wife of Dr. Robert Schuller, pastor of the Crystal Cathedral, shared this grandmothering story in the book *Friends for Life* by Jim and Sheila Coleman. One night Arvella agreed to baby-sit her daughter Sheila's four rambunctious boys, ages one through four. As Sheila and her husband, Jim, rushed to get out the door on time, they hurried through last-minute instructions about diapers and bottles and emergency phone numbers. "Oh, yes," Sheila added, "here's the medicine for Nicky's bronchitis. Give him a teaspoonful before he goes to bed."

It was a hectic evening, but Arvella didn't forget the medicine. Nicky made a terrible face and fussed a lot, but she forced the medicine into his mouth. When he tried to spit it out, she held his lips shut until he swallowed. Figuring it wouldn't hurt to check the bottle just to be certain the dosage was correct, Arvella made a horrible discovery. She had given baby Nicky the dog's medicine!

Horrified, she called the poison control center, only to be put on hold. When someone finally came back to the phone, he suggested Arvella call the vet. The story does have a happy ending. The medicine was only a combination of vitamins. There was nothing harmful in the concoction at all. In fact, when Arvella called Sheila the next morning to check on Nicky, Sheila responded cheerily, "Well, I checked him over this morning. His hair is pretty shiny, his nose is wet, and he's been barking orders at me ever since he got up!"

You say you aren't the kind of grandmother who can do it all? We don't know of one who can. Certainly neither of us fits that description. You say you make grandmothering mistakes? Join the crowd!

## Grandmothering Is Hard Work!

Grandmothering is an awesome adventure. Here we are, smugly thinking our days with children are behind us, when we find ourselves plunged right back into the hectic lifestyle of kids. To keep up, we need the energy of a twenty-year-old, the resources of a kindergarten teacher, the creativity of a camp director, the patience of a saint, and the fitness of an aerobics instructor. To anyone who asks, we gleefully insist, "Oh, but I love it!" And we do. But our bodies keep protesting, *Give me a break!*

We want to do it all. In our hearts, we are determined to be the person who will make a real and lasting difference in the lives of our precious grandchildren. Only thing is, we're not sure our bodies can keep up with the convictions of our hearts.

Jan says that when she and Dave have all of the family

together, she loves it but it wears her out. "I've tried to detach myself from time to time to get a break," she insists, "but somehow I end up superinvolved in everything going on. I have a hard time knowing what my limits are."

Betty's family had just left after a great two-week visit. All three daughters and four grandchildren were in town. She held up amazingly well, despite the endless activity, the constant going and doing. "My hand was in everything," she admitted. "I saw it as my responsibility to pull it all together, to keep everything going and in balance." She did a great job. Only thing was, the minute the last ones got on the plane, Betty drove home and was dead to the world for the next several days. "I didn't want to answer the phone," she said. "I didn't want to make a decision about what to eat or what to wear. I didn't want to get out of bed." The adrenaline had pumped hard for two weeks, but when *it* stopped, *she* stopped. "I can't think straight," Betty said. "I can't even put together a sentence until I take time to regroup. It was never like this when I was a mother."

Well, we have changed, haven't we? Our energy reserves are certainly not what they used to be. But then, the situation is different too. When we're with our grandchildren, we focus totally on them. We put every bit of our energy into it. We wear ourselves out. It wasn't that way with our own children.

If we can learn that we do not have to do it all, we can actually enjoy our time with our grandchildren, and they can enjoy us. The answer is not to do more, but to act more wisely and more in keeping with who we are. Again, we grandmothers are called upon to perform a most challenging balancing act—staying actively involved while consistently letting go.

"I'm learning to plan ahead in order to better enjoy the

time I have with my grandchildren," Jan said. "Each day we're together, I remind myself that this isn't going to be our only time together. We don't have to do it all today. Realizing this takes the pressure off."

You may be saying, "That's all well and good for grandmothers who have their children living close by and who get to see them often, but I seldom get to be with mine. When we are together, I have to make the most of it." You're right. It is harder for long-distance grandmothers. You need to develop other strategies. (We'll provide other tips about long-distance grandparenting in Chapter 16.)

Betty shares this suggestion: "When my family was visiting, I should have chosen several times during the two weeks to withdraw and let my daughters take over. I felt I needed to give them an unbroken vacation, but I really didn't have to do that. The next time I will take time to lie down when I'm tired, read a book, and go off by myself and recharge."

It is this type of drawing back and recharging that will allow you to carry on without wearing out. Plan ahead for times and places to withdraw. Choose not to take full responsibility for everyone and everything. It's perfectly all right to say, "Grandma needs to take a rest now."

One problem with us grandmothers is that we think we are so critical to every situation. *But I have to be here,* we think. *It can't get done without me.* It's downright painful to discover that our families can get along quite well without us doing it all! They do survive without our help. And when we take care of ourselves, we're more effective during the time we're together. The fact is, taking the time to pull away and being careful not to overdo makes us better grandmothers. "I have explained to my daughters that I need space and some time alone," said Betty.

It's our responsibility to arrange for what we need. Our

children, and certainly our grandchildren, aren't going to arrange it for us. If they tried, most of us would resent it. We don't want others telling us we're tired, that we need to lie down. We want to be in charge of ourselves.

### Different Gifts, Different Styles

"I am a terrible cook," one grandmother told us. "I'm not one to make my house smell of delicious things when my grandchildren come over. I don't even cook for my husband and myself anymore. I feel guilty that I'm not the homebody type of grandma."

Another said, "I keep all kinds of art and crafts supplies in my garage cupboard. When my grandkids come over, they just can't wait to find out what project we're going to do this time. I love it too. We have so much fun together! But sometimes things get out of hand and the kids get really silly and rowdy, and I tend to lose my patience. I wish I could be a little more tolerant of their roughhousing."

"I can't do a thing with my hands," admitted another grandma. "Crafts are great for other grandmothers, but I don't know where to begin. What I like to do is get down on the floor and play games with my grandchildren. We don't care how silly other adults might think we are. We just have fun together!"

Are you a great cook and baker? Are you creative at arts and crafts? Are you fun and innovative at playing games? Are you a wonderful storyteller and book reader? Are you a gifted musician? Are you an exciting teacher who can make facts spring to life? Most likely you answered yes to at least one of these. But all of them? And at the same time? Probably not. Certainly neither of *us* can. We all have our gifts, but none of us is gifted in every area.

One grandmother who was trying to do it all said, "Whenever my son calls and asks if I am going to be around for the weekend, I always say yes because I so value my time with little Aaron. Whatever I have on my schedule gets crossed off. I make cookies, I go to the park, I play hide-and-seek for hours, I read until I am hoarse. When he leaves, I collapse. What am I doing wrong?"

Instead of trying to do everything, it would be helpful for this grandma to learn to concentrate on the things she really enjoys doing with Aaron and then to let the other things go. It won't be easy; Aaron has gotten used to having his grandma do everything with him. But by cutting back, Grandma will be able to be a more relaxed, more loving grandmother.

## Finding Your Style

Each of us has a grandparenting style, a special way of giving loving support and nurture that fits us perfectly. Our challenge is to find that particular style and work from within it.

We have found that grandmothers fall into one of four main styles, which we call *discover, doer, dreamer,* and *director.* No one style is better than another; it is just different from the others. Each style brings with it specific strengths and abilities as well as potential pitfalls. Once you know where you fit, you are in a position to maximize your strengths and to avoid the pitfalls.

To help you determine your particular style of grandparenting, we have developed the following questionnaire. Rank each of the four possible responses to each statement in the order of your preference (write 1 by the statement that is most important to you, 2 by the statement that is next in importance, 3 the next, and 4 the least important). As you go through the questions, don't worry about how you're doing. There are no right or wrong answers here. At the end of the questionnaire we will tell you how to compute and chart your responses.

## Grandmothering Style Questionnaire

1. When your grandchild becomes an adult, which of these compliments will give you the greatest satisfaction? "My grandma taught me

____ A. how to solve the problems in life by paying attention to reality."

____ B. how to relate to other people and care about them."

____ C. how to analyze things in creative, innovative ways."

____ D. how to be consistent in the details of my life."

2. The characteristics I value most in myself are that I am

____ A. realistic and direct, one who loves jumping into a task and getting it done.

____ B. warm and feeling, one who values close and nurturing relationships.

____ C. inquisitive and objective, one who is able to see the big picture and longs to learn more and more.

____ D. patient and hard-working, one who gets a lot of satisfaction in an efficient and well-planned way of doing things.

3. It is important that my grandchild learns

____ A. useful skills that will help him succeed in life.

____ B. how to get along with other people and be empathic.

___ C. how to question things and decide priorities.

___ D. leadership skills and how to respect authority.

4. It is usually difficult for me to

___ A. sit and wait while someone tells me how to do something.

___ B. focus on a task I need to do right now without being distracted.

___ C. understand someone else's emotional response to situations.

___ D. adjust and adapt to a lot of changes.

5. It is important for me to

___ A. have options.

___ B. know that others like me.

___ C. never make the same mistake twice.

___ D. be organized.

Now look back at the way you ranked the four statements under each point. Do you see a pattern emerging? If you ranked all or most of the A responses as 1, you are a doer-style grandmother. If you ranked all or most of the B responses as 1, you are a dreamer-style grandma. If you ranked all or most of the C responses as 1, you are a discoverer-style grandmother. If you ranked all or most of the D responses as 1, you are a director-style grandmother.

If there is no clear pattern, add up the points you gave to A (doer-style) answers, B (dreamer-style) answers, C (discoverer-style) answers, and D (director-style) answers. The *lowest* score will be your strength, the next lowest score will be your backup style, and the highest score will be your weakest area. Record your results on the chart below:

My strength is the _____ style. (lowest score)

My backup is the _____ style. (next lowest)

My weakest area is the _____ style. (highest score)

So now you know your style. But what does it mean to you as a grandmother? That's exactly what we will be discussing in depth in the next chapter.

## Chapter 6

# Grandmothering in
# Our Own Style

*G*randmothers don't have to do anything, just be
there. They are old, so they shouldn't play too hard
or run too fast." That's what a six-year-old wrote. Great
advice for us fast-moving grandmas! We want to do it all,
but instead we could learn to relax and learn to do more of
what we *really* enjoy and less of the things we *think* are
expected of us.

The two of us are good illustrations of the differences
that occur between even the most dedicated grandmas.
Let us tell you a bit about our own grandparenting styles:

Jan is a dreamer. *Creative* is her middle name. Her main
concern when her grandchildren are around is that they
have fun.

Betty is a doer. She is much quicker to get things done
and she's more involved in *active* play.

"When I was going to take my grandchildren on a two-
week trip, I bought two or three things for them to do in
the car," Betty said. "But Jan helped me by coming up
with something for them to do every single day—games,

toys, all kinds of fun things. The kids have never forgotten it."

"I get excited about ideas," Jan said. "I dream it all out but I never seem to get around to getting it done. Betty does. She catches on to ideas quickly and gets the job done and does it well!"

Jan-the-dreamer is sensitive; Betty-the-doer is forthright. Jan entertains; Betty accomplishes. Jan dreams it out; Betty gets it done. That's us. Now let's look at you.

To develop our descriptions of grandmothering styles, we've pulled together ideas from several sources, including the Myers-Briggs Type Indicator, a test used by psychologists to identify personality types. See if you can find your grandmothering style in the following profiles.

### Doer Grandmothers

"My grandkids love to come to my house because we are always doing something," one grandmother reported. "There's no sitting around here! We love to go to the park, take walks, go to the store, cook things, make and paint and put together. Sure, we like to read stories and do the quiet things, too, but the kids and I both do better if we have something active planned. I don't have a lot of patience with them when they whine and say they don't know what to do."

Spoken like a true doer grandma.

Doer grandmothers are practical, down to earth, and realistic. They are "now" people. For doers, today is to be lived and enjoyed. Some people may call them impulsive, but in reality these grandmas are just responding to their need for action. "I don't need to plan," a doer might say. "I need to act!"

If you are a doer grandmother, you are affected by what

you see, hear, and touch more than by what you feel emotionally. This doesn't mean you aren't a person of deep feelings. On the contrary, you are capable of intense emotions. It's just that what you take in through your senses is so important to you that it colors everything you feel and think.

Because you are so affected by the things you pick up through your senses, you pay close attention to what is going on in your environment. This observant nature gives you the ability to stay on track with a task once you have started it, especially if the task is tangible and clearcut.

When asked what she liked to do with her grandchildren, one doer grandmother said, "Just keep it practical and specific!" *Specific* is a good word for this style. You doers want people to give clear and exact instructions. If they do, you will make it work. (You notice we didn't say "detailed" instructions, because this is one of your pet peeves. "Get on with it, get it done, and don't bother me with the small stuff"—that's your slogan.)

## Gifts of the Doer Grandmother

Doer grandmothers are great at keeping children's attention and interest. By definition, doers seem to have an endless supply of energy that allows them to do all kinds of spontaneous things. Picnics and outings? They are a treat for both grandmother and grandchild. Active play? Swimming or hiking or playing ball? They are great fun. Doer grandmothers also love to do hands-on projects such as crafts and art that can be finished relatively quickly.

While doers want others to be specific about tasks, they don't want to be told *how* to do anything. And they don't often *need* to be told because they are good at figuring it out for themselves. Problem-solving is one of their main gifts.

A surprise advantage of this style of grandmothering is that a doer's attention span tends to be about the same length as her grandchild's. About the time the child begins to feel bored with a project, Grandma is getting pretty tired of it herself.

Doer-style grandmothering helps children learn that today is to be enjoyed and experienced. One young woman whose grandmother was a doer told us she had learned from her grandma that nothing is impossible, that there is always a way to fix anything. "As a result, I've figured out how to do many things my friends simply gave up on," she said. "What a gift that I-can-fix-it attitude has been!"

Doer grandmothers are never bored with life—unless their options are taken away. They aren't boring to be around, either, for they can be excitingly unpredictable. Their attitude is up and positive. Doers can give their grandchildren a sense of confidence about life that is indeed a great gift.

### Limitations of the Doer Style

Perhaps a doer grandmother's biggest struggle is patience, especially when she is faced with a problem that could have been avoided. Doers tend to be short on empathy as well. It's not that doer grandmas don't care, it's just that it's so very frustrating to have their fun spoiled by something that didn't need to happen in the first place.

While doers are good at finishing short projects, they are often bored by those that are long or drawn out. Organization isn't strong with doer grandmothers. The doer style is loose and flexible—arrangements that serve the purpose but aren't too involved. Doer grandmas are much better at spontaneity than at long-range planning. Plans made too far into the future make them feel tied down.

### Dreamer Grandmothers

"When my grandchildren stay over with me, we do all kinds of special things," one grandmother told us. "I fix all the foods they love to eat. At night when we go to bed we lie in the dark and make up silly songs. Then I tell them stories until they drift off to sleep. They love to sleep over with Grammy."

Grammy is a dreamer grandmother through and through. Dreamers want the kids to have fun. The kids make a mess? It's okay. Grammy will clean up after they are gone. They want to use the sewing machine? Sure! Cook dinner? Bake bread? Finger paint? Sure! Dreamers want to let their grandchildren experience it all. They want to fill in all the gaps.

Dreamer-grandma Jan loves to take the down comforter off her bed and spread it on the floor. Then she cuddles up on it with her granddaughter and they pretend they are on a cloud. "We just go wild with our thoughts," she said. "We make up stories about what we see way down on earth."

Imaginative, independent, intuitive—a dreamer grand-mother is all of these. She is the "tomorrow" person, always looking to the future with all its possibilities. She sees all sides of any project or problem—she sees the big picture.

Dreamer grandmothers believe it's discouraging to have someone say, "Let's be realistic about this," because that usually means they're going to get bogged down in facts. They know facts are important, but they say, "What is more important is how people *feel*."

If you are a dreamer grandmother, you show a lot of feeling and put a high value on your relationships, including your relationship with your grandchildren. You are empathetic and intuitive. But if other people are out of the picture for very long, you are apt to feel lonely, maybe even depressed.

## Gifts of the Dreamer Grandmother

Dreamer grandmothers are especially good at reading and telling stories to their grandchildren, especially stories that are different or unusual. They throw themselves into it, changing voices for the different characters and really getting excited about the story. Dreamers are also good with arts and crafts. This artistic flair may take the form of acting, as grandmother and grandchild make up stories and act them out. "Let's-pretend" playing fits the dreamer style well.

Another natural activity for dreamers is sympathizing and comforting. Could the hurt a child caused himself have been avoided? It doesn't matter. The important thing is that a child is hurting and needs to be held, hugged, kissed, and made to feel better. When someone is hurting it's never time to teach a lesson, the dreamer asserts. Often a dreamer grandmother can sense the emotional needs of her grandchild even before the child is fully aware of his or her own feelings.

Growth, both intellectual and emotional, is important to dreamer grandmothers. They don't want to see any stagnation on the part of their grandchildren. So their activities together often have a meaningful focus, but one in which the children are free to explore. Most of all, dreamer grandmothers are fun.

## Limitations of the Dreamer Grandmother

If you are a dreamer grandmother, you have probably been made keenly aware of your physical limitations. You try to do too much and you end up frazzled and worn out. What you may not have understood is your tendency to extend yourself emotionally beyond what you are able to provide. There is a sense in which dreamers offer more of themselves than they can give.

Because the dreamer grandmother is so tuned in to the emotions of her grandchildren, it is sometimes difficult for her to set limits and boundaries between herself and them. Saying no to a child can be a real problem. At the same time, a dreamer grandma can become so involved emotionally she has difficulty staying objective in situations regarding her grandchildren.

Dreamer grandmothers expect a lot from others, including their grandchildren, but not nearly as much as they expect from themselves. If they are not careful, their good qualities can leave them worn out and drained dry.

### *Discoverer Grandmothers*

"My grandmother wasn't much to express her feelings toward me," an adult granddaughter told us. "What I most remember about her is her garden. She was a wonderful gardener, and she gave me my own little plot and bought me my own little tools. Gently and lovingly she would tell me about the plants we grew, the birds that flew overhead, the rabbits that came to nibble in our garden. I learned so much from her. To this day, gardening is a major part of my life."

What a great picture of a discoverer grandmother. Discoverers are the ones who have collections. Their seashells are mounted, their collections are sorted, they have butterflies drying in the kitchen. *Teaching* is their byword.

"My grandson and I have great fun investigating and learning about all kinds of things," one discoverer grandmother told us. "We have many projects going, like a rock collection, butterflies hatching on the laundry porch, and leaves drying so we can see how the different ones turn out. I think studying about things and looking things up in the encyclopedia are so important for a child."

Discoverers want their grandchildren to learn about things and to learn to do things. And they want them to learn *right*. Playing a game? Great, but it had better be played by the rules. Making a model? Wonderful. But it must be accurate.

Principles and competence are important themes to discoverers. They grow impatient with redundancy, and even more impatient with incompetence. Of all styles, discoverers are probably the ones who are hardest on themselves.

Discoverer grandmothers want their grandchildren to have cultural experiences—plays, museums, the planetarium, the zoo. They try to expose their grandchildren to different things. This style grandma might plan an international meal for which everyone dresses up in costumes. Maybe she will take her grandchildren shopping in Chinatown, being sure to stop and watch the fortune cookies being made. And all the while she's teaching.

If you are a discoverer, you are a teacher at heart. You want to expand your grandchildren's understanding of the world.

Competent, curious, intelligent, perfectionistic—these are good words to describe you. You may lack confidence at times, but if so, no one will ever know it. When we look at you, we see a self-assured, in-control person. You like things in order and tasks accomplished efficiently. Logical and analytical, you want to understand things. People may sometimes think of you as insensitive, but you aren't. It's just that at times you tend to be so analytical and logical you overlook the feelings of others.

If you are given a task, you usually know what to do even without consulting the instructions (which you usually find boring and redundant anyway). You like to plan, predict, and figure things out on your own. But unlike the doer grandmother who rushes to the finish, you put great value on getting the job done right. Accomplishing competently and developing a great curiosity about knowledge, these are matters of great value to you.

## Gifts of the Discoverer Grandmother

Because of their focus on intellectual activities, discoverer grandmothers are wonderful, natural teachers. They encourage their grandchildren to explore and investigate and figure things out for themselves. They teach them to delve deeply into a project, do it well, and enjoy learning from the experience.

Because discoverers see play as an opportunity to learn, games and activities usually have some educational angle to go along with the fun. Competition is great, but to win, their grandchildren must beat them fair and square.

Like the dreamer, the discoverer is concerned with the meaning of things. Because she looks at the larger picture, she will help her grandchild see why things are done a certain way, then guide them in considering creative ways to get them done.

Because they are taught to see and follow a logical order and strategy, discoverers' grandchildren grow up with a sense of confidence and integrity.

## Limitations of the Discoverer Grandmother

Discoverer grandmothers may not be the warm, snugly grandmas. They don't usually do the "touchy-feely" things naturally. A cuddly grandchild may have trouble relating to a grandmother he or she perceives as somewhat cold and objective. Some discoverer grandmas do well when they become aware of this and remember to practice hugging and cuddling.

While teaching is one of the discoverer's greatest gifts, it can also be a liability, for she tends to see everything as a lesson. She doesn't get into play just for the sake of playing many times, or just kick back and have fun. A kid who just wants to be a kid can easily be overlooked by a discoverer grandma. And because doing things right is so important to her, a discoverer may find it difficult to let her grandchild struggle through a project without jumping in and "doing it right."

Because of her strong emphasis on the intellectual side of life, a discoverer grandmother may find it hard to focus on the feelings of her grandchild. It's not that she doesn't care; it's just that she's not as tuned in to this side of life as some other styles are. Empathic understanding isn't her strength. As a result, an emotionally close relationship with her grandchildren might not come easily. Instead, their closeness will more likely be based on their mutual discoveries and understanding of the world around them.

## The Director Grandmother

"I just can't stand how disorganized it is at my daughter's house," a grandmother told us. "My grandchildren aren't learning the basics in life. They don't even know how to fold their own clothes or anything. When they visit me, I feel it's my job to add some semblance of order to their existence. I try to teach them things that will help them get along in life. But I try to make it all so much fun they want to do it. We make a game out of cleaning up and setting things straight. Of course we do all the other fun things, too, like reading and playing games, but we have little routines for everything. When my grandchildren are at my house, they are so well behaved. I just don't understand the chaos they live with at home."

These are the words of a director grandmother. Organized, in control, traditional, good at teaching, the director-grandmother has patience with routine and detail like no other style of grandma. She maintains organization by her ability to teach and direct. Sometimes a director will overpower others with her need for organization, but in the long run, the others turn to her for stability and guidance.

If you are a director grandma, you probably know the feeling of being habitually overworked. You see so much that needs to be done, and you tend to take a lot of responsibility upon yourself.

In any situation you like to know what the rules are and where the boundaries are drawn. You find comfort in knowing you will get proper instructions when you are given a task, and being the kind of person you are, you will probably follow them. You do your work promptly and well, and you are irritated when others don't do the same. Like the grandma in the story above, you can't understand why they wouldn't want to.

Director grandmothers are the traditional ones. Holidays are wonderful at their houses because the celebrations are rich with history and traditions. There is a natural stability in carrying on the traditions, in doing the same things in the same way. There is a continuity to it, a dependability. It's comforting and comfortable—until the director runs headlong into someone else's spontaneity. The bane of director grandmothers is grandchildren who want to break out of the mold and change the schedule.

## Gifts of the Director Grandmother

Director grandmothers have a wonderful ability to plan and organize. And this gift that allows their projects to run smoothly also sets them up for a smoothly flowing life. As directors thrive on organization, they help their grandchildren learn to organize their own lives, even when it isn't a natural part of the child's personality. Because of Grandma, the grandchild learns to plan ahead and pay attention to detail, to be responsible and accept his or her duties, all skills that will prove valuable throughout life.

Because family history and tradition are highly valued by this style of grandma, she invariably instills a desire in her grandchildren to take up those traditions and keep them alive.

Like the discoverer grandmother, the director is a natural teacher, although the two have different teaching styles. For the director, traditions play as important a part in the lesson as does the information itself.

A director grandmother carries along to her grandchildren a natural stability that gives the kids a strong sense of

security and safety. Her style of life is one that her grandchildren will treasure for years to come.

## Limitations of the Director Grandmother

How are you at dealing with confusion and change? If
you are a director grandmother, you will almost certainly
find this frustrating. Directors have a difficult time adjust-
ing to chaos within their families. It is the director's strong
belief that everyone could be as organized as she is if they
would only try. Other people's disorganization and the re-
sulting confusion are a major part of her frustration. If a
director's grandchild is not naturally interested in organization, Grandma will be frustrated with that child.

If you are a director, it is important that you recognize
organization as one of your great gifts. You can impart
some organizational skills to your grandchild, but it is un-
likely that he or she will ever be as competent at it as you
are.

Dealing comfortably with intrusions or changes in
schedules is another struggle for the director grandma. She
may take them as a personal affront and withdraw from
her family. Flexibility and making adjustments to unwel-
come interruptions are good areas for her to develop.

Because director grandmas so value responsibility,
when they see someone dropping the ball, they tend to
rush in quickly to pick it up. Once again, the director ends
up doing much more than her share and becomes overbur-
dened with responsibility—and quietly resents it. It's too
much of a good thing.

### How about You?

Wouldn't it be nice to be able to claim the strengths of
all four grandmothering styles? Unfortunately, it doesn't

work that way. Yet some of you have been trying to excel in everything.

Good news! The joy of grandparenting comes when we can recognize our strengths and limitations, then learn to live within them. For more information about personality styles we recommend the following books: *Type Talk* by Otto Kroeger and Janet M. Thuesen, *Gifts Differing* by Isabelle Briggs Myers and Peter B. Myers, and *The Intimacy Factor* by Dr. David Stoop and Jan Stoop.

Now that you know your own particular style, give yourself permission to release those areas that are not your strengths. It will be a wonderful relief.

It will be wonderful for your grandchildren, too. No child wants a frustrated grandma, worn out from trying to do and give too much. In fact, if that's the kind of grandmother you are, your grandchildren are likely absorbing frustration and weariness from you. Instead, be a grandmother who knows her limits and her strengths. That type of grandmother will be free to explore the many gifts all grandmothers can give their grandchildren. It is those gifts—the gifts of grandmothering—that we will be looking at in Part 3 of this book. And as we do so, we will discuss how you as a doer, dreamer, discoverer, or director grandmother can maximize your strengths and minimize your weaknesses.

The gifts of grandmothering will include the following:

***The gift of self-value.*** By building our grandchildren up, we are laying a foundation that will allow them to be all they can be.

***The gift of listening.*** Listening is the very foundation of communication, yet for most of us it is our least developed skill. It is vital that we really listen to our grandchildren.

***The gift of sharing history and traditions.*** Our

family stories and traditions are too valuable to be lost. And the process of passing them along can build a special bond between us and our grandchildren.

***The gift of holiday times and creative ideas.*** Making holidays memorable and ordinary times special will take creativity on a grandmother's part.

***The gift of time and money.*** These twin pressures of today's society are gifts we can give our grandchildren— even those of us who don't have much of either.

***The gift of support.*** What should a grandmother do in times of crisis? How can she best offer support, and when is it right to intervene? There are guidelines to follow.

***The gift of wisdom.*** Knowing what to do and when to do it can be one of the most important gifts we grandmothers can give our grandchildren.

***The gift of sharing God.*** It is possible for us to offer spiritual guidance to our grandchildren without slipping into "preaching."

You may choose to read straight through Part 3, or you may decide to focus on the gifts that are particularly important to you. Either way, we urge you to recognize the wonderful gifts you have to offer and be ready to share them with your grandchildren.

*Part 3*

# *The Gifts of Grandmothering*

# Chapter 7

❧

# The Gift of Self-value

The photo studio was packed with mommies in line and kids everywhere. While Betty's daughter waited her turn to see the proofs of pictures taken the week before, Betty rode herd on Elizabeth, her just-learning-to-walk granddaughter. As they played and laughed together, Betty noticed a black-haired little girl of about four. Although the child stood alone across the room, her huge dark eyes never left Betty and Elizabeth.

"Hi!" Betty said to the little girl. "What's your name?"

The child dropped her head, shuffled her feet, and mumbled something softly.

"What?" Betty asked. "I didn't hear you."

The little girl shyly mumbled again. Betty still couldn't make out her answer, so she just smiled at the child and turned back to play with Elizabeth. That's when the little girl's demeanor suddenly changed. She raised her head and called out in a voice strong and clear, "But Grandma calls me Precious!"

You, dear Grandma, do make a difference. And perhaps the most important difference you make is at the vital foundation of helping to determine how one very special child—your grandchild—feels about himself or herself.

Betty's Grandmother Eichenberger ("We called her Grandma Ikey") was one grandma who knew how to quietly and unassumingly construct a foundation of feeling good about oneself. Grandma Ikey, the mother of eight children, lived on a farm and worked hard her entire life. She had neither the time nor the money to indulge her grandchildren. But she knew each of them—really knew them—and she respected each one for who he or she was. This attitude came through even though they rarely did anything together that others would consider special. In return, every one of Grandma Ikey's grandchildren respected her and held her in high esteem. She didn't cuddle much, but, oh, how she loved. She didn't have a sugary way of talking, but she conveyed to each grandchild the firm belief that he or she would turn out okay.

The first question on our questionnaire was, "What did your grandparents mean to you?" The most frequent answer we received was, "Grandma meant unconditional love."

All of us have a rock-bottom-basic need to feel good about ourselves. Without that, how can we hope to really give love to others or to accept it from them?

One woman wrote this tragic statement on her questionnaire: "My grandparents didn't speak to me until I was twelve years old because I wasn't a boy." Another said, "My sister was my grandmother's favorite and Grandma showed it every day in many subtle ways." Contrast these statements with the woman who told us, "Ah, Grandma's house! That was the only place I could go where I didn't feel like the dumb middle daughter."

Unconditional love—or rejection? You may not think your deepest feelings show, but they do. And, oh, the difference an attitude can make for the rest of your grandchild's life. Being one step removed from the responsibilities and daily routine of parenting, we grandmas are freer to instill in our grandchildren that priceless feeling of unconditional love and acceptance.

## Love and Logic

Love and logic—these two areas are vital if we are to be successful at building up our grandchildren. Sure, most parents can and do provide both of these things as well. But often parents' logic seems to take precedence over their demonstration of love. The result is that children get the distinct feeling they will be loved *if* they follow their parents' logic.

Because we don't bear the responsibility of having to raise the children and discipline them, we grandmas are freer to love our grandchildren "just because." We can let them know they are people of great value, wonderful, one-of-a-kind individuals created by God.

We mean a lot to our grandchildren. So simply by showing them that we firmly believe they are people of worth who deserve happiness, achievement, and love, we are laying a solid foundation for their respect of themselves.

Still not convinced you're the one who can do it? Consider this statement by Arthur Kornhaber and Kenneth L. Woodward in their book, *Grandparents/Grandchildren, The Vital Connection:*

Emotional attachments between grandparents and grandchildren are unique. The normal conflicts that occur between children and parents simply do not exist between grandchildren and grandparents. This is because grandparents, no matter what they were like as parents, are exempt from the emotional intensity that characterizes parent-child relationships. The common view that grandparents have all the fun of being a parent and none of the responsibility is based upon a profound psychological truth that has become evident in our research. . . . There-fore, grandparents and grandchildren are naturally at ease with each other while both have intense emotional rela-tionships with the middle generation.

In a cartoon we saw recently, two little boys were watching a ball game on television. One said to the other, "Maybe the reason they play so well is that they don't have parents yelling at them from the sidelines."

We can be the ones who don't yell from the sidelines. We can be the ones who care nothing about hits or misses. We can leave the logic behind and focus on the love.

## Setting Boundaries

Unconditional love doesn't mean there won't be bound-aries. Without them, life would be chaotic. Yet boundary setting—learning to determine boundaries and to enforce them—can be a real problem for grandmothers who are concerned about loving their children and helping them feel good about themselves. Let's look at how the various grandmothering styles might approach this important area.

### The Doer Grandmother

Boundaries do not come easy for doers. They tend to let things go and forget boundaries altogether until things get completely out of hand. Then they reach their limit and that's it! They can literally explode into a boundary. The problem with this approach is that it isn't fair to the chil-dren. They don't know where the boundary is until they crash headlong into it.

If you are a doer, your challenge will be to consciously determine ahead of time where the limits are, then to communicate those boundaries to your grandchildren.

## The Dreamer Grandmother

The dreamer grandma may set even fewer boundaries than the doer grandma: Her emphasis is on fun, and boundaries and fun don't seem to fit together. (There are more rules when Mom and Dad are around, however, because Grandma wants to keep them happy, too!) The dreamer's boundaries can be nebulous and lax. After all, she has high expectations and she feels sure everything will turn out the way she plans. But since nothing ever quite seems to meet a dreamer's lofty expectations, Grandma is bound to be disappointed.

Dreamers usually don't think in terms of rules. They love spontaneity. For them, rules are made to be broken. No wonder dreamer grandmas are famous for letting their grandkids get by with anything. (And no wonder they are so often taken advantage of!)

## The Discoverer Grandmother

A discoverer grandmother usually has rules. She knows just how things are to be done. Her boundaries are more clearly defined than a dreamer's and more organized than a doer's, but they are somewhat flexible as well. Still, there can be a certain condition to them in that a discoverer grandmother's attitude is often *If you're going to violate the principles, I'll have to withhold something.* They are so busy teaching a grandchild that they forget to hand out the warm fuzzies.

A discoverer's boundaries may not always be clearly

spelled out to the children. Still, most children find it fairly easy to work within them. When they do know what's expected of them, they also know the rules can be bent a bit if the circumstances warrant it.

## The Director Grandmother

For a director grandmother, there is no question as to where the boundaries are. Grandma has spelled out the rules, and rules are to be obeyed. Freedom and spontaneity don't always fit.

Rambunctious grandchildren who can't stand structure won't do well within a director grandmother's boundaries. In fact, unbendable rules can cause conflict between most any grandchild and his or her grandparent.

Director grandmothers struggle the most with unconditional love because they have so many conditions in their own lives. For them love is earned because "you're expected to," "you're supposed to," and "you should."

If you are a director grandmother, just being aware of your tendency to make your love conditional will enable you to guard against doing so. For you, follow-up is important. After coming down hard on a grandchild who has broken the rules, go back and temper the reprimand with a softer kind of love: "We won't talk about the mess any more. Come on, I'll help you clean it up."

### Grandma Logic

The grandparents' logic is not the same as the logic of parents. Foster W. Cline, in an interview in the *Bottom Line Personal* newsletter, described love and logic from a parent's standpoint as love that is not permissive, that doesn't tolerate disrespect and that is powerful enough to allow them to make mistakes and to live with the consequences of those mistakes. Logic has to do with the consequences of our children's mistakes. If we let our children live with the frustration, disappointment and pain that logically follow their mistakes, they will learn from the mistakes.

As grandparents, we can be somewhat more permissive in our love. We can allow our grandchildren some freedom or special privileges they may not be allowed at home. We may even jump in and try to keep them from making mistakes.

Grandma logic, gained through years of experience, understands that some of the rules and regulations we set for our own children were more for our needs and expectations than for the good of our kids. Armed with that knowledge, we are freer to have fewer rules and regulations for our grandchildren. Certainly this doesn't give us permission to undermine their parents' guidelines. But it does allow us to leave the strict disciplining to the parents and to bask in the freedom of a more relaxed relationship.

### *It's Never Too Early to Start*

Laying the foundation for healthy self-confidence in a child can begin at birth. Remember the thrill of holding your tiny grandbaby for the first time? Remember all the emotions that sprang to the surface? Remember the overwhelming realization that that baby was a part of you, that your hopes and dreams were focused on that tiny child?

Tell that child how you feel. Even if he or she is still a baby, express your love and delight out loud. Even if the baby doesn't understand a word you say your words will still have a positive effect. It's the way you speak them that will communicate your loving acceptance.

"My grandmother always sang to us," Betty recalled. "When I came home after my first child was born, Grandma was there, and she immediately began singing and talking to my baby. That pattern continued through the years. I have chosen to follow Grandma's example. I sing and talk to my own grandchildren—silly little made-up songs, family lullabies, Sunday school songs, whatever comes to my mind or fits the situation. They all give a feeling of closeness and security, and that's what counts."

Another way to reinforce the uniqueness of your grandchildren is to have a special "pet" name for each one. Florence Littauer, a popular speaker and writer who travels most of the time, has done this. As she travels from place to place, she keeps her eye out for cards or little items that include the pet name of any of her grandchildren. She sends the little gifts to the appropriate children or brings them with her when she returns home. This lets each child know that even when Grandma is busy or away, she is still thinking of that child.

Knowing that "Grandma calls me Precious"—or Princess or Kitten or Sport or Amigo or whatever—enhances a child's sense of security and value and worth. Jan likes to use these special names in songs she sings to her grandchildren. "I call them wonderful names in the songs and sing about who loves them." One time Jan was rocking two-year-old Colleen to sleep. Thinking the child had drifted off, Jan stopped singing. After a few minutes Colleen looked up at her grandma, then softly took up the song and finished it with her own little made-up tune and words. "I guess she figured I was too tired so she would have to finish it!" Jan said. "It made me realize how important my singing was to her."

### *I Don't Want My Grandchild to Be Conceited . . .*

Don't confuse a healthy sense of self with prideful conceit. The importance of feeling good about oneself is well known throughout the psychological world. Dr. Nathaniel Branden, author and clinical psychologist, says in an interview with *Bottom Line Personal* (June 30, 1991), "Healthy self-esteem is a basic human need. It is indispensable to psychological development, . . . to resilience in the face of life's adversities . . . to our feeling of belonging in the world . . . to our ability to express joy."

Even a strong sense of self cannot protect a child from the trials and difficulties of life. But it does give that child the resiliency to endure them. Interestingly enough, it may also serve as an immune system of sorts. A child who feels secure and loved by his or her family and by God is not as susceptible to dangerous peer influence. Several adults told us the very fact that their grandparents trusted them was a deterrent to the temptations that arose at crucial times during their growing-up years.

### *But I Do Want My Grandchild to Be Confident*

Throughout your lives together, as you relate to your grandchildren you will either be building them up or tearing them down. Dr. Maya Angelou was named woman of the year by *Ladies Home Journal* in 1992; she is also the recipient of thirty-five honorary doctoral degrees and has been named as one of the top ten most influential, positive black women of the twentieth century. Dr. Angelou told a gathering of women at an international women's conference that she is the woman and leader she is today because of the gifts her grandmother gave her simply by her presence and her actions. At the age of seven, Maya Angelou was raped. She told the authorities the name of the rapist and they went after him. Word quickly came back that the rapist had been kicked to death in the streets. With the logic of a seven-year-old, the child decided her voice had killed the man. She didn't speak again for almost six years!

Her grandmother, who raised her, would brush her hair and say, "Sister, Mama don't care what these people say about you being an idiot and a moron because you don't talk. Mama knows when you and the good Lord get ready, you're gonna be a preacher."

Dr. Angelou said she would sit there and think, *Poor ignorant Mama. I'll never speak again, let alone preach.*

But her grandmother didn't give up. She took the child to church with her and continually told little Maya, "Sister, you're going to be a preacher."

Her grandmother's persistence and belief in her is responsible for her speaking and writing today, Dr. Angelou maintains. And she said, "I thank God for my grandmother who stood on the Word of God and lived with the spirit of courage and grace."

Luci Swindoll—author, lecturer, humorist, and former corporate executive—was at the same conference. She said her grandmother had imparted to her the importance of a good sense of humor: "My grandmother used to say that a day is wasted if you don't fall over at least once with laughter."

Your grandchild may never grow up to be a Maya Angelou or a Luci Swindoll. Then again, who knows? Whoever and whatever our grandchildren grow up to be—yours and ours—let's do everything we can to make them the most powerful, the most well-adjusted people they can possibly be. Let's covenant to do everything in our power to help them reach the pinnacles God planned for them.

# Chapter 8

❧

# *The Gift of Listening*

*W*hen our youngest daughter, Kristi, was six years old, we moved into a new house where she would have a bedroom of her own for the very first time," Betty recalled. "Though we did everything in our power to discourage it, Kristi insisted she had to have a waterbed. We reasoned and argued and gave her every excuse we could come up with, but she was determined. Finally we simply told her no, she could not have a waterbed, and the subject was closed.

"Kristi's grandmother, who had overheard many of our discussions with her, quietly wondered why Kristi was so adamant about that waterbed. Gently, she began to probe. As they were talking one night, it finally came out that Kristi had seen a friend's house burn down, and it had made her deathly afraid of fire. 'If our house catches fire,' she told her grandma, 'I could just punch a hole in my waterbed and put the fire out.' Grandma told us the problem, and we worked together on ways to ease Kristi's fears," Betty said.

What wisdom Kristi's grandma showed! Not so much in her suggestions for a solution to the problem, but in taking the time to listen to what her little granddaughter was feeling.

Throughout the Bible we are encouraged to open our ears that we might hear. We both realize that during our parenting years our children said many things to us we never heard. No, neither of us has impaired hearing, but evidently our listening skills could have used some improvement. Now that we are grandmothers, we are pleased to announce our listening has improved greatly!

One of the most precious gifts any grandmother can give her grandchildren is the gift of really listening to what they have to say. In responding to our question, "What did your grandmother mean to you?" one woman wrote, "She was a wonderful listener." Hooray for that grandma!

## The Art of Communication

Most of us recognize communication as the key to building a strong relationship. Yet listening, the very foundation of communication, is our least developed skill. Strange, isn't it?

How do you listen? Some grandmothers take in just enough information to allow them to give this kind of off-the-top-of-the-head response:

JOHNNY: "Grandma, I hate school!"
GRANDMA: "Oh, Johnny, school is good for you! You don't hate it."

This grandma is simply hearing the surface statement her grandson has made and quickly reacting to it. Suppose instead Johnny's grandmother were to respond with a question:

GRANDMA: "Can you tell me what it is about school you
   don't like, Johnny?"
JOHNNY: "It's too hard. Anyway, nobody likes me."

Good. Grandma is getting into the problem. But now
she has to resist the temptation to offer a quick-fix response such as this:

GRANDMA: "You're a smart boy, Johnny; you can make
   it. And I know everybody likes you."

An answer like this, well-meaning though it may be, ne-
gates the very real feelings of the child. So what will a listening grandma do? She will ask questions that go beyond
the surface:

GRANDMA: "What is it that seems too hard? What happened that makes you think nobody likes you?"

By listening sensitively to what the child is saying, by
tuning your ear to hear what is *not* being said, and by responding appropriately to both, you have a good chance
of opening up the underlying issue that needs to be recog-
nized and addressed.

For awhile, when Jan's granddaughter Michelle spent
the night with her, Michelle invariably fought bedtime.
She seemed to be afraid to go to sleep. Jan read to her, held
her, sometimes even let her climb into bed with Grandma
and Grandpa, but still Michelle seemed frightened. Jan
fought against the temptation to keep urging Michelle to
talk about what was bothering her, even though it seemed
it would be helpful for her to talk. At a later time, when
she felt more comfortable talking about it, Michelle told

Jan about her terrifying dreams of a child-eating monster that roamed the streets trying to get her. In the dream, when Michelle ran away from the monster and escaped into a house, the lady who lived there would at first let her in, but then the dream lady would tell Michelle there wasn't any child-eating monster out there, and she would send Michelle right back out on the streets.

After listening carefully to her granddaughter's dream, Jan asked her questions about both the dream and her feelings. Then she asked about school, about her friends, and about home. Michelle could tell Grandma was really listening to her

Jan and Michelle began to talk about the real reason Michelle was afraid. Jan knew all about Michelle's new baby sister at home. Michelle's real fear, it turned out, was that she might no longer be important in her family's busy life. Although she had never before expressed these fears, night after night they were being played out in her dreams.

Jan found that when she took the time later to really listen to Michelle's dreams and fears, and was willing to talk honestly about them with her, Michelle was able to voice her real fears—and then face them. "I found when I jump in too quickly or suggest answers for her, she shuts down and our communication stops," Jan said.

A child needs to be heard—*really* heard. "My children often chided me because I was such a busy mother I never stopped what I was doing to just sit and listen to their daily trivia," Betty admits.

Giving others our undivided attention is one of the richest gifts we can give. "I remember well the hurt I felt when our teenage daughters gave up trying to come home and share with me what was happening to them on a daily basis," said Betty. "They sought out others who would give them the undivided time and attention they needed. I said I was listening, but by continuing with what I was doing, I was conveying to them that they were not as important as my work.

"As a grandparent, I can now see my own daughters following in my footsteps. They listen, but they keep on with their 'busy-ness.'"

Jan finds she is so busy doing different things that she easily gets distracted by her own thoughts when she should be listening more completely to a grandchild. "I am learning from my daughter-in-law, who is a great listener," she said. "I now reach down and touch a child who is trying to get my attention, and I let that touch say, 'I'm not ignoring you. Your turn is coming.' This simple gesture gives the child the reassurance that he or she will get a chance to speak, and he or she doesn't have to keep asking."

Parents today have demanding schedules. We know from experience how difficult it is to stop and listen to what the kids have to say. But this is a gap we grandmothers can fill. We can be available to give our grandchildren our total attention.

Certainly this is more of a challenge for you grandmothers who live far away from your grandchildren. You have to be more creative and more persistent. One grandmother told us, "I give what I call 'call-me cards' to my teenage grandchildren so they can call me any time." Another said, "I write them often and I always include a blank note card, addressed and stamped, for their reply."

## Traits of a Good-Listener Grandma

To our survey question, "What do you wish could have been different in your relationship with your grandparents?" one lady answered, "I so wish we could have had more meaningful conversations. Instead of so much work, work, work, I wish there had been more talk, talk, talk. I would have gladly traded more time for fewer meals."

It's not easy to be a listening grandmother, but, oh, it is so rewarding! Grandmothers who are good listeners share some of the common traits we list below. If you recognize these in yourself, congratulations! You are definitely on the right track. If not—well, now you have some idea where you need to concentrate your efforts.

## 1. A good-listener grandma tries to hear the feelings behind the words that are spoken.

Tone of voice, body language, facial expressions—these are often clues to what is really going on in the child. Sometimes, after a child has repeatedly been told, "You shouldn't feel that way," his or her emotions are bottled up, become disguised, or are even shut down completely. When this has happened, a grandmother must work very hard at trying to discover the feelings behind the words. If this sounds like your grandchild, take time to ask questions, then listen sympathetically to the answers.

A friend of ours has a seven-year-old grandson we will call Steven. One evening little Steven was curled up in a ball in the corner of his grandparents' living room, muttering something under his breath. Grandma tried to talk to him, but he wouldn't respond. Finally Grandma lay down on the floor beside Steven and wrapped her arms around him. Quietly she listened and waited and waited and listened. As her ear became attuned to Steven's muttering, she realized what he was saying: "I hate me! I hate me! I hate me!"

Grandma's heart broke for her little grandson. She had

just opened her mouth to say, "Oh, no, Steven, you mustn't feel that way!" when she thought about all the turmoil that was going on in the little boy's home. She was well aware that he was often disciplined for his constant disobedience. She also knew his parents were having marital problems; his dad had moved out the weekend before. Could it be that Steven was feeling responsible for his parents' problems?

Gently Grandma began to talk to Steven. She reaffirmed her love for him. She spoke of his goodness and his specialness. As Steven slowly relaxed, he began to sob. Grandma held him and let him cry until he was ready to start telling her what he was feeling. Grandma asked questions, then patiently listened to what Steven had to say. He was convinced his parents' marriage breakup was all his fault. By hearing the feelings behind the words "I hate me" Steven's grandmother discovered his true feelings. She followed up with the second step in good listening:

## 2. A good-listener grandma echoes what she hears.

Have you ever heard the statement, "I know you believe you understood what you think I said, but I am not sure you realize that what you heard is not what I meant"? Confusing, isn't it? But too often it's true of grandmothers and grandchildren. If you take the time to rephrase the words your grandchild has spoken and repeat those words back to him or her, it gives the child the opportunity to correct any "mis-hearings" you may have had. This is called "active listening." Not only does active listening require you to check out the accuracy of what you have heard, it also requires you to concentrate more on what the child is saying than on how you are going to respond.

By patiently repeating in her own words what she thought she heard Steven saying, Grandma was following step number three:

### 3. A good-listener grandma resists the temptation to jump in with a quick-fix.

Jumping in with good advice is our natural reaction to any problem our grandchildren have. But resisting the urge to shower them with the benefit of our great wisdom is the sign of a good listener.

By taking the time to listen for feelings and echo back what we hear, we enable our grandchildren to see and understand more clearly what is going on in their lives. This helps them learn to take the steps necessary toward solving their own problems. By asking questions, you show them you are really interested and attentive to what they are saying. Because this is a compliment to your grandchildren, their response is likely to come more readily.

Some of us are especially tempted to overwhelm our grandchildren with spiritual and scriptural answers, many of which can come across as frustratingly pat to them. Instead of listening to what the kids are saying, we spend our time watching for an opening where we can jump in and present our own point of view. There's nothing wrong with sharing your point of view and your wisdom. It's an important part of teaching—if you wait for your grandchildren to ask for it and if you have listened enough to earn the right to share it.

### 4. A good-listener grandma knows her limits.

One of the dangers of being too good a listener is that you may find yourself becoming a dumping ground for everyone's sad stories and bad experiences. Sometimes our need to be needed can cause us to fall into the trap of moving from being a good listener to simply being a co-conspirator in misery. Good communication is a two-way street. There is a time to listen and there is a time to speak. If your grandchild is always dumping problems and trials into your listening ears without hearing what you have to say and then seeking his or her own solutions, it's time to set some limits.

Every time something went wrong at school, or whenever her parents punished her, Louanne would call her grandma to complain. Grandma was so pleased that Louanne took her into her confidence that she gladly commiserated with her. But as time went by, Grandma discovered the only time Louanne ever called was when she wanted to complain. Her negative thoughts and feelings were beginning to depress Grandma. She found herself dwelling on all the unfair things poor Louanne had endured, and becoming more and more angry at her son and daughter-in-law for the "unfair" punishment Louanne was getting.

Before long, a tension began to develop between Grandma and Louanne's parents. At family gatherings, Grandma and Louanne would sit off to the side, making negative comments about everything. By now, Grandma had become as negative as Louanne. In time, Louanne's calls to Grandma became less frequent. Feeling sorry for herself, Grandma started calling Louanne to complain about this and that. But things had changed. Louanne had a boyfriend now, and her closeness with her grandmother was fast becoming a thing of the past. Since she wasn't interested in Grandma's negative comments anymore, Louanne simply avoided talking to her.

The problem with Louanne's grandmother wasn't that

she didn't care for her granddaughter. It was that she didn't know her limits. In her desire to be needed, she fell into the trap of alienating others by listening to—and encouraging—Louanne's self-pity. When we don't set boundaries, we stop being helpful.

### 5. A good-listener grandma has to work at it.

Learning to be a good listener takes commitment. Not everything our grandchildren tell us is deep and important. If we are to be good listeners, we must commit ourselves to listening to all the trivial stuff they chatter about.

One woman said the most important thing her grandmother did for her was to "treat me as if my thoughts really mattered." What a legacy for a grandmother to leave!

#### *Moving On*

Good communication starts with developing good listening skills, but it doesn't stop there. Communication between grandmothers and grandchildren means taking the time to be aware of the world in which our grandchildren are living. This may mean learning something about the music they listen to, the movies and television programs they enjoy, and the mores of their peers. We need to ask them about their special interests and be teachable when they answer us.

Betty's grandson Timothy is a sports nut. As the mother of three un–sports-minded daughters, Betty knew almost nothing about Little League, football, or soccer. "Communicating with Timothy means I ask about all his different sports," Betty said. "I do my best to attend his games when I'm visiting him. I ask him to be my teacher and explain the game to me."

A grandma with a teachable spirit shows interest in what interests her grandchildren, and in doing so she sets them an example of being interested in others. Our grandchildren are wrestling with concepts we knew nothing about when we were their age. One wise grandmother wrote, "It's a whole new generation. Even though I'm a baby boomer, I am still surprised at how rapidly society is accelerating. So I ask. My grandchildren and I talk about sex, jobs, careers, relationships. Nothing is off limits between us."

As we learn about our grandchildren's world, we can adjust our examples and advice specifically to them. Instead of saying, "When I was a girl, I . . ." we can begin to say, "Perhaps a good way to handle that situation would be . . ." And there's a bonus for us: We gain from learning about the young people's world. It is new knowledge and understanding that keeps us alert and growing.

Be honest in your communication with your grandchildren. When you don't understand their position, their behavior, or their point of view, let them know, then be ready to listen as they try to explain. When you cannot accept their point of view, don't preach at them or condemn them. Simply let them know how and why you see things differently than they do. Children need role models with strong standards, people who are willing to firmly, calmly, and honestly stand up for their principles. You can be such a person for your grandchildren. (Understand that many times children are simply testing the ideas they have picked up from others. This is a normal process of growing up. Allow your grandchildren the respect of knowing you listen to their ideas, ask questions of them, and then lovingly share your perspective on the situation.)

Sometimes the ideas or actions of our grandchildren are so shocking to us we react without thinking. Betty's father did that when his beloved grandson Bruce showed up sporting an earring in his ear. Grandpa blurted out his shock, then launched into a lecture on how disgusting earrings were on men. Grandpa didn't want an explanation on why Bruce had chosen to wear an earring. All he wanted was for Bruce to get rid of it, pronto!

But after the initial shock had worn off, Grandpa realized there was really nothing he could 'do about Bruce's earring. He still loved Bruce and would say nothing else about the earring. But if Grandpa is to keep the lines of communication open, he needs to ask Bruce why he chose to wear an earring, then he needs to listen to Bruce's reasons. He doesn't have to agree, but he does need to hear his grandson. That spontaneous outburst and lecture cannot be ignored. Unless it is dealt with, it will forever be a barrier to Grandpa and Bruce's communication.

Let your grandchildren know that, while you may not always agree with them, you will always be there to listen and share. Provide a safe place where they can come and share their joys and their sorrows, their fears, failures, and successes, knowing you are there to hear their every word. Being available to listen and communicate with your grandchildren may be both the most difficult and the most important thing you will ever do as a grandmother.

# Chapter 9

### ❧

# *The Gift of Sharing History and Traditions*

*G*randma, tell me a story. Please? Tell me about the olden days when you were a little girl." We don't know of a grandmother anywhere who hasn't heard this plea. And except for the part about the "olden days," most grandmas love to respond.

Some of Jan's favorite memories are of her own mother telling her stories about the grandparents who died before Jan was born. To this day she remembers how far they walked to school, carrying their shoes so they didn't wear out too quickly. "I want my own grandchildren to remember those stories too," Jan said. "They are a vital part of who we are as a family."

Stories and tales of the past can be an important tie between grandparents and grandchildren. Grandmas love to tell them, and grandchildren love to hear them. And through the stories, grandmas have a wonderful opportunity to teach their grandchildren the uniqueness of their family history, culture, and traditions.

You say you aren't a creative storyteller? You say your family is so ordinary there really aren't any stories to pass along? Ah, no, that isn't so. Each and every one of us is unique. We may tell stories differently, but we can all tell them. And each of us comes from a unique family. When you look back and search into the past, you will almost certainly make exciting new discoveries about yourself and the family members who have gone before you.

Because your stories are far too valuable to be lost, consider putting them down in written form for your grandchildren—and generations after them—to enjoy. One excellent way to do this is to build a memory book.

## Building a Memory Book

There are many ready-made books available to help you with this. All you need to do is fill in your own facts and stories. *Grandmother's Precious Moments, Special Memories for My Grandchild* is an excellent one. Published by Thomas Nelson, this beautiful book has wonderful illustrations by Samuel J. Butcher, the creator of Precious Moments figurines.

Of course, you don't have to buy a ready-made book. We have a friend who, with the help of her children, created one for her mother to fill out. She collected all the questions her children asked about their grandmother's past and added other basic questions that might arise. Then she purchased a three-ring notebook, filled it with blank pages, and titled each blank page with a question for Grandma. Armed with scissors, paste, and a pile of old magazines, mother and the kids spent many afternoons finding just the right picture to fit each question, cutting the pictures out, and pasting them on the appropriate pages. When the pictures were in place, the grandchildren gave the book to Grandma to fill in.

You could do something similar with your grandchildren, telling them the stories as you work together on each page. It would be an especially good ongoing project for you to work on whenever they come to visit you.

### *Your Grandmothering Style*

Some of you may already be gathering up your scissors and paste. Others of you may be preparing for a trip to the bookstore to see what's available there. Or you may be thinking of a completely different method of making a family record. Whatever way you decide to proceed, your grandmothering style will likely influence your approach to the project. Let's take a look at the differences in the ways the four styles are likely to proceed:

If you are a *doer grandmother,* you will likely attack the project impulsively. When the idea strikes you, you drop everything and start. For a while you work compulsively on it, then you get tired and set it aside. The greatest problem is that once it is out of sight, it is also out of your mind. It will help if you make it a point to set your project aside in a prominent place so you can't forget it.

If you can discipline yourself to periodically pick it up, your fortunate grandchildren will get a thoroughly finished memory book.

If you are a *dreamer grandmother,* you are probably already bursting with all kinds of wonderfully creative ideas about how your book will be put together. Maybe you are planning captions and little comments to write beside each picture. Certainly you will enjoy making it very personal. But you, of all grandma styles, will have to struggle the most with the temptation to set it aside and never pick it up again. Your best bet is to get your grandchildren excited about doing the book with you. If it becomes a fun project for them, too, you will want to go back to it and work on it with them. And what fun you will all have!

If you are a *discoverer grandmother,* you will be excited about the learning possibilities for your memory book. What an opportunity to demonstrate the things you have learned by experience! What a chance to introduce your grandchildren to relatives and ancestors they will never know in person! And if you are careful to make it fun as well as instructional, how your grandchildren will love the learning. You discoverers won't have to worry about getting your book done. You're great at completing projects.

If you are a *director grandma,* you will approach the book methodically, step by step, working consistently at a scheduled time each day. Not that you will work compulsively; you won't. But you will hold to a realistic time frame, and you will get it done. Traditions will play an important part in your family memory book. And what better way to hand down those traditions, to explain where they came from and what they mean? If you are careful to add some creativity, you will have a wonderful legacy to give your grandchildren, a family book they will cherish for years to come.

Different approaches, yes. But whatever your style, your grandchildren can end up with a real family treasure.

## So What Should I Put in My Book?

Do you need some help getting started? If so, here are some ideas for stories and facts you might include in answer to questions children typically ask:

## Grandma, where were you born?

Besides the actual place you were born, you might include the hospital (or home) and the date. How about setting the time in history ("That was two years before the Japanese bombed Pearl Harbor")? You can also share some descriptions of the setting to help the place come alive ("My father always said it was the coldest place on earth when the wind blew. That December . . .").

## Tell me about when you were little.

What an open question! Here you can tell your whole name and how it was chosen. (Don't forget your nicknames and how they came about.) You might want to list the names of your parents, grandparents, and great-grandparents, and tell a little story about each one. Don't forget your brothers and sisters and their places in the family. It would be fun to add baby photos of yourself if they are available. Some things that would make interesting stories here are: What kind of birthday parties you had. What a typical winter day was like for you. How about a day during summer vacation? Did you have pets? If so, tell about them. What were your jobs around the house? (Don't be afraid to share your childhood disappointments and hurts as well as your happy memories. This is a good opportunity to teach your grandchildren that those, too, are a part of life.)

## What did you do for fun?

Tell about your favorite toys and the games you liked to play. Did you have television? Did you go to movies? What were your favorite books? Don't forget to share stories about your friends and the silly and funny things you did together.

**What was your house like?**

Describe the house where you grew up and include any pictures you might have. If you moved many times, share those experiences. Be sure to include the loneliness or fear you felt as you moved to new schools and neighborhoods. This could help your grandchildren express their own uneasiness about some similar situations they may be facing. Here are some other questions you might answer: Did you have your own bedroom? What was the bathroom like? How about the kitchen? Did you have a fireplace to keep you warm? Did you have a secret hiding place? Did you have an attic or a basement? What was kept there? How did you keep cool in the summer and warm in the winter? Did firemen or policemen ever come to your house? Did anyone other than your immediate family live with you?

**What was your school like?**

Tell what your school was like and how it differed from the schools your grandchildren attend (now or in the future). If you have kept some of your childhood schoolwork or report cards, it would be good to incorporate them. You can also answer such questions as, Did you like school? How did you get there? (This is your one appropriate opportunity to say, "When I was your age I had to walk miles through the rain and snow"!) What classes and teachers did you like? Why? What did you hate? Did you get good grades? Did you participate in sports? Were you in any school plays? Did you ever play hooky? (And what does "hooky" mean, anyway?) What did you do at recess?

**Were you ever naughty?**

Children often have a hard time visualizing adults as ever having been their size or feeling what they feel. Sharing times you were punished and how you were disciplined, times you ran away (or wanted to), times you were scared or angry, can give your grandchildren openings to share their own secrets or feelings with you.

**Were things different then?**

Share stories of the ways in which times have changed. It might be fun to look for pictures of automobiles or other modes of transportation that were common when you were a child. Describe your family cars—what kind they were and how much they cost. Tell about methods of communication. (Your grandchildren will find it hard to believe that you can remember the days before computers and VCRs!) Paste in pictures of you dressed in the styles of different periods of your life. (Your grandchildren will get a good laugh. You may, too!)

**Did you go on vacations?**

Besides telling of your childhood vacations, include vacations you took when your grandchildren's parents were young. It's fun to remember fishing and camping trips, a train trip, your first airplane ride or boating adventure, what Disneyland was like the first time you visited. This is a good time to get out a map or globe and chart the different places you have visited. (You discoverers will especially enjoy this opportunity to teach about history and geography, as well as about social relations.) As you work, you can ask your grandchildren about their favorite vacations or their dreams of where they would like to travel. This might also be the place for those picture postcards you picked up years ago and couldn't bring yourself to throw away. They can be wonderful illustrations of the places you have been.

**What was Grandpa like?**

Your grandchildren will also want to hear about your experiences with Grandpa. How and where did you meet? How old were you, and how old was he? Did Grandpa have any rivals for your affections? Where did you go on your first date? Did you like him right away? Did he write you love letters? Did you ever fight or get mad at each other while you were dating? What did your parents think of Grandpa? When and where did he ask you to marry him?

"Michelle loves to hear her grandpa tell about his relatives who still live in Nothern Ireland," said Jan. "She made a report to present to her school class on Dave's uncle who is the pastor of a church on Shank Hill Road in Belfast where so much of the fighting has taken place. The stories of the warmth of hospitality in the homes there and the wonderful cooking help her to picture what life is really like in Ireland. I think it gives a child a sense of permanence to know her roots can be traced way back across the ocean."

You may want to include your own wedding pictures in this chapter. Talk about your feelings of excitement and any fears or doubts you may have had preceding your wedding. Who was in your wedding? Where were you married? What did you wear? Where did you go on your honeymoon? Where was your first home? Tell of your early life together: the jobs you both had, the church you attended, the places you went and things you did. This might be a good opportunity to discuss finances, budgeting, and learning to handle money wisely.

If your marriage didn't work out, this may be a place to show by example the importance of looking beyond emotions and into the reasons for the choices we make. Again, it should be a time of honest reflection and sharing with the child. Be very careful that instead of venting your hurt or anger from a painful past, you simply point out where you made mistakes and how you have learned from them.

## What were Mommy and Daddy like when they were little?

Children love to hear stories about their parents when they were young. As you give the information, use baby pictures and other memorabilia you have saved through the years to illustrate the pages. Talk about discovering you were pregnant or your excitement over an adoption. Share those first memories of where and when your child was born and what your feelings were. Was the baby easy to care for or was he or she fussy? How did you decorate the nursery? What did you feed your baby? Did the baby suck his or her thumb or use a pacifier? What was he or she like as a child? What were the favorite toys? When did he or she start to walk and talk?

Having their parents included will make the memory book all the more fun for your grandchildren.

## Your Teenage Grandchildren

As your grandchildren approach their teen years, they are less likely to ask you questions. They will be more interested in the opposite sex than in your history. You may recapture some of their attention by recalling for them your first dating experiences. How old were you before you could date? Who was your first date? Where did you go and what did you do? How late did you stay up? Who was your favorite boyfriend? Other questions about your adolescent years you might want to address are: What did you and your best friend do together? Did you work when you were a teenager? What did you do for fun? Did you have a special nickname? What made you angry? What caused friction between you and your parents?

If you have pictures of yourself during that time, it will be fun to compare the clothing and hairstyles of those days with what your grandchildren wear today. Teenage girls are fascinated by styles of the past. (Many of those styles are being recycled in fashion today, by the way.) This may give you an opportunity to talk to your grandchildren about appropriate dressing and why what you wear says so much about you. But do be careful: This is the time to discover and understand, not to lecture or make judgments.

Perhaps reliving your own teenage insecurities will help you open the doors of communication with a teen who is going through difficult times.

## A Chapter for Each Child

Perhaps your grandchildren have some special passions in life. For one it may be music, for another, sports, for another, computers. Another child may love the outdoors or may have a deep affection for horses or dogs. Whatever the passion, go back into your history and see if you can find something you were passionate about that might help you relate to each child specifically, then put together a chapter on that subject.

Is your grandson always glued to his Walkman? We know, we know, he probably listens to some musical group you can't understand and certainly don't enjoy. But try to remember back to the music that was popular in your youth. Maybe somewhere you still have a record or two from that era. The point here is not to condemn your grandchildren's choices, but rather to share how and why you listened to your own music back then (that your parents and grandparents probably thought was terrible!). Talk about certain songs and the memories they bring back. Who were your favorite singers and songs? Did you take music lessons? If you went to dances when you were young, do you remember your first dance? If you recall the music or songs that spoke to something deep within your spirit back then, perhaps you can better understand how the music the kids are listening to today is speaking to something deep within them.

## And More about You

At the end of your memory book, you may wish to provide more information about yourself, such as giving a list of your favorite things: color, book, movie, actress, song, radio program, television program, ice cream, soup, sandwich, toy, hobby, spectator sport, participation sport, vacation place, cookie, restaurant, city, actor, game, bird, flower, pet, candy, month, season, tree, magazine, cartoon, automobile, vegetable, time of day, dinner, and so forth. You may also wish to include funny family stories, poignant and thought-provoking stories, stories of family get-togethers, and a list of where all your relatives are living now.

## *You Don't Have to Do It All Today*

Worn out just thinking about it? Don't be. This certainly isn't a project you should plan to tackle and complete in an hour or two, or even in a couple of days. Anyway, it will have more meaning if you make it into an ongoing endeavor. Even if it isn't possible to work on the project with your grandchildren, it is still well worth taking the time and trouble to set down the record of your history. If making a book just isn't for you, try using an audio or video recorder and put your stories down on tapes.

Keep your eyes open for meaningful ways to supplement the stories in your memory book. One woman told us about a grandmother who did this so well. "Grandma had a lovely old cedar chest her mother had given her as a child, and because I was her oldest granddaughter, she always told me I would get it," the woman said. "The summer I was ten, I spent a week with her and together we sanded down the chest. All the time we sanded, she told me the stories of every little nick and scratch. I have had the cedar chest for twenty-eight years now. Someday I will pass it on to my granddaughter, along with all the stories behind it."

## *The Gift of Traditions*

In a mobile society such as ours where families move, on the average, every four years, traditions can easily get lost in the shuffle. Remember Tevya, the great philosopher of *Fiddler on the Roof* who longed for the security of tradition? Our grandchildren, too, need the roots of tradition to give them stability in this ever-changing world.

Parents are often too busy (or too "enlightened") to bother with traditions. Yet the fact is that in each of us there is a longing for how things used to be. It may be that when your kids were growing up, you were too busy to incorporate traditions from your and your husband's backgrounds. You don't have to let them die. It's not too late to dig around and resurrect some of those traditions.

If you don't have family traditions, create some traditions of your own. They certainly don't have to be elaborate or expensive. It was traditional in Betty's family to take a photo of each child on the first day of school every year. Another tradition in her house is that out-of-town grandchildren always have a little package or surprise waiting for them each morning they are there. One grandmother told us it was traditional in her family to put lost teeth into a glass of water beside the bed rather than under the pillow. The next morning the lucky child got to "dunk" for money from the tooth fairy.

French toast on Saturday mornings is a tradition in Jan's family—not just any French toast, mind you, but Grandma's French toast. Grandma Hes made up the special recipe and taught it to Jan, who in turn has taught her children. Now her son Mike is teaching his daughter the special recipe. Jan says that often in a restaurant the children will look at the menu and say, "Look, they have French toast that sounds like Grandma's, but I know it doesn't taste like hers!"

Many traditions have their origins in ethnic backgrounds. You might want to research typical traditions from your own ethnic culture and begin to institute some of them into your family gatherings. If, like most of us, you are a blend of backgrounds, it may be fun to incorporate a different tradition from each culture on special occasions throughout the year.

Certain traditions come and go, and need to be changed as the grandchildren grow older. When Betty's little two-year-old granddaughter comes, Betty greets her with, "Who's heeeere? Who's heeeere?" It's great today, but may wear thin by the time the child is seven. When she's thirteen, she won't want any part of such a childish game.

One woman told of her bread-baking grandmother. "When my sister and I walked into her house, Grandma would always cut the hot heels off her fresh-baked bread and melt butter on it for us. Whenever I smell fresh-baked bread, I think of Grandma." And it has become a tradition, for on the first day of school each year, her own children are treated to fresh-baked bread heels dripping with melted butter.

Another woman told of a time she was out of town when her small son lost a tooth. "Be sure to put money under his pillow," she reminded her husband over the telephone. When she arrived home her son proudly announced, "Look what the tooth fairy gave me: a quarter, two dimes, three pennies, and a San Diego bus token!" What started with a fatherly tooth fairy emptying his pockets has become a tradition. Now when a child loses a tooth in that family, he gets money plus a surprise—a fancy button, a stick of gum, an old key.

Both dreamer and director grandmothers are by nature more tradition oriented. But director grandmothers have a much harder time being flexible and shifting over if something doesn't work: "We should have Swedish rice pudding for Christmas Eve dinner, even if nobody likes it because that's what we've always done." Dreamers may have ideas for new traditions, but those ideas are not firmly set in their minds: "I always dreamed it would be this way when I had children, so I just know there is some way to make it work." If you are a director grandma, you will find your family traditions running more smoothly if you inject some flexibility into them. If you are a dreamer, focus more on objectives and think of other ways to reach your goal.

Discoverers and doers are all for finding new things and trying different ways, or maybe just for challenging the old ways. "Just because we've always done it like that doesn't mean it's the best way," they say as they set out raspberry whipped-cream dessert in place of the traditional Swedish rice pudding. Established traditions aren't nearly so important to them, though for different reasons.

They try something and if it works, great. If not, they try something else. The difference is that the discoverer is always asking, "Why?" and the doer is always saying, "Let's not be boring!" The challenge for you discoverers and doers is to keep that secure foundation of tradition alive. Be flexible, but don't be too quick to discard the way it's always been done.

Whatever your grandmothering style, traditions and history are important. With a sense of transience undermining families today, who we are and how we do things and where we came from can still carry through the generations. As Tevya knew so well, tradition helps a child become a whole, well-adjusted person, anchored in who he or she is.

As we grow older and see our parents and aunts and uncles dying, we so wish we had asked more questions. Even if your grandchildren aren't asking now, the time will undoubtedly come when they will look over the written legacy you have left them and they will rise up and call you blessed.

## Chapter 10

# The Gift of Holiday Times and Creative Ideas

*I*t was Easter morning. Betty and Fred herded their three preschoolers into a local hotel to have breakfast with grandparents, great-grandparents, and aunts and uncles before church. The morning had not started off well. The children were cranky at being awakened so early. They fussed and cried about having to have their hair curled and combed. Why did they have to get all dressed up anyway? they demanded. Who wants to wear a fancy dress with a scratchy petticoat and a funny hat with flowers on it?

Betty knew this early breakfast in a fancy restaurant wasn't a good idea, but she felt pressured by her family's insistence that they be there. Fred was no help at all. He thought it was stupid to expect three little girls to awaken early, dress up, and sit still for a twenty-minute ride to a restaurant where they would be expected to behave like well-mannered little adults while being handled and cooed over by well-meaning relatives. As if all that wasn't enough, breakfast would have to be rushed if they were to get the children to church in time for their small part in the Sunday morning program.

By the time the family arrived at the restaurant, the children were in tears and Betty and Fred were barely speaking to one another. The tension continued to build as the children squabbled and whined through breakfast. Betty, torn between the demands of her family and Fred's insistence that they take the children and leave, tried desperately to keep everyone happy. Finally Fred jumped up from the table in anger and frustration, gathered up the crying children, herded them into the car, and headed home. Betty was left behind, confused, hurt, and angry.

Holidays. Not all the memories they conjure up are good and happy and uplifting. Have you ever endured a holiday where the family's expectations and demands were so rigid the occasion turned into a time of anger, hurt, and disappointment? What a tragic loss of what should have been a joyous family occasion.

## Saving the Holidays

What can we do to help make a holiday special without turning the event into a frustration of rigid expectations? Let's look at some ways a wise grandmother can make this happen.

### Consult the Parents

Resist the temptation to make plans and set expectations that involve your grandchildren without first talking the matter over with the children's parents. Make it a rule to discuss your plans and ideas with them, asking them for their feelings and reactions.

One of the toughest areas of parenting and grandparenting is learning to release plans, hopes, and dreams about the way special occasions should be done. Your adult children's plans for their family may not include doing things your way. It may even be that their plans won't include you at all.

As our children marry and start their own families, they take on new obligations and begin traditions of their own. A grandmother who wants to continue being a part of the special family times needs to be sensitive and open to the changing times and different ways. When you discuss your ideas, be careful not to present them as demands. Make it clear you are willing to listen to other ideas. This attitude will help set the stage for harmonious family holiday gatherings.

## Clarify Your Role in the Celebration

When you consult your children about holiday plans, make sure you understand what role, if any, they expect you to perform. Only after you have done this are you free to proceed with your plans. You may be disappointed with the time or position allotted you, but this is not the time to voice your complaints. Rather, this is your chance to demonstrate your maturity by making the most of the time you do have. When we make the most of our opportunities, we are likely to find that our opportunities increase.

The holidays most likely to present conflicts are the major ones, such as Thanksgiving, Christmas, Easter, July 4, and family birthdays. If you have been limited to very little direct participation in these holidays, look for other days you can make special for your grandchildren.

Betty's mother made a major tradition out of May Day (May 1). When her grandchildren were too young to help,

Grandma made simple May Day baskets filled with goodies and flowers, and hung them on doorknobs. She knocked on the door, then ran and hid. Even little toddlers loved to open the door and find a special basket there just for them. As the children grew older, they were invited to help make the baskets out of such homey materials as strawberry baskets woven with strips of colored construction paper. Children ran to the garden to pick flowers for the baskets. For hours, little hands were kept busy coloring and creating and decorating and packing those special gifts of love. Betty recalls what fun it was to distribute those baskets to friends and neighbors, ringing their doorbells then hiding in the bushes to watch the delight of the lucky people who got them.

Some grandmas enjoy working side by side with their grandchildren, making and creating festive decorations for holiday occasions. Others prefer to take the children shopping for special gifts. Others love spending hours in the kitchen preparing meals, baking cakes and cookies, and making candy with the grandchildren.

Jan recalls the day she and Michelle tackled the project of unpacking the box of Thanksgiving decorations. In the bottom of the box Michelle found some old cookie cutters in the shapes of turkeys, pilgrims, and Indians. Her eyes lit up. Jan knew they were in trouble because there was only an hour until Michelle had to be home. "Could we make Thanksgiving cookies, Grandma? Please? Just a few? Real fast?" Michelle begged. Jan hesitated, but Michelle was so insistent she agreed to try.

"They came out beautifully," Jan said. "We sent some home with Michelle, and everyone agreed they were some of the best cookies ever. I know why. They were made by two people who love each other and the time they have together."

Other grandmothers might want to research the history of certain holidays and share the stories with their grandchildren. (If you cannot do this in person, try recording the stories on a cassette tape and sending it to the kids.) The thing is, we need not be limited to our own personal creative abilities. Some of us find it hard to think up fresh, new ideas for making the holidays special. So, what's wrong with adopting the ideas of others and tailoring them to meet the specific needs of our families? What you do is not nearly as important as the fact that you do something. Just sending a card with a quarter or a dollar enclosed tells your grandchildren you are thinking about them, and that they are special to you.

There are many books available that offer specific instructions on special activities children and adults can do together. Two excellent ones are *Grandmother Time* by Judy Gattis Smith, and *Let's Make a Memory* by Gloria Gaither and Shirley Dobson. *Grandmother Time* is filled with stories, activities, and games for grandparents and children. *Let's Make a Memory* focuses on holidays, seasons, and special places.

## Holiday Gifts

Another big question often pops up at holidays and on other special occasions: "What will I give the grandchildren?" Here are some considerations to help you decide.

### Toys

In his book *Rosemond's Six-Point Plan for Raising Happy, Healthy Kids,* John Rosemond, a family psychologist, writer, and father, says a good toy embodies the following qualities:

1. It is safe and durable.
2. It presents a wide range of creative possibilities. (That is, it can be used in many ways, its capabilities defined only by a child's imagination.)
3. It can be taken apart and put together in various ways.
4. It is age appropriate. (Most manufacturers list age ranges on the boxes.)

Rosemond especially praises classic toys produced before 1955 such as blocks, electric trains, dolls, and marbles. "I noticed that my children had the most sustained interest in the same toys I played with as a kid, such as Lincoln Logs™ and Tinkertoys™," he said.

## Games

We have noticed with our own grandchildren that the toys that are the latest fads, the ones constantly being touted on television and talked about by children in the neighborhood, are the ones that, no matter how much they have been begged for, very soon end up sitting unused on the shelf. Toys that have stood the test of time in our households include the Fisher-Price line of "little people" with the accompanying garage, school, town, airplane, farm, and so forth. These are toys our children played with, and now our grandchildren continue to enjoy them. Also successful are such games as Chutes and Ladders®, Hi-Ho! Cherry-O®, Candyland®, and checkers. For older children, such games as Sorry®, Monopoly®, and Uno® provide hours of fun.

Because kids enjoy playing the same games over and over, investing in good games and teaching grandchildren how to play them is money and time well spent. It is also a perfect opportunity to help children learn how to be good winners and good losers, and how to be good sports.

## Books

Good books are another excellent investment. "My grandmother was always willing to buy me the latest Nancy Drew mystery book," Betty recalls. "She encouraged my reading. Today, reading is one of my favorite pastimes."

Jan keeps special books in a "cubby hole" under the stairway just for her grandchildren, and little Colleen loves to get them out. Her favorites are pop-up books small enough to fit in her little two-year-old hands. "She 'reads' them to me and sometimes to our dog, Molly," Jan said. "When she climbs up on my lap and crosses her feet, I know she is ready to listen as I read to her."

If your grandchildren have discovered authors they especially enjoy, encourage their love of reading even though you may not think those authors are the most talented writers around. When you have given the children books they enjoy, they will likely be willing to try a book you suggest as one of your favorites. Betty's reading tastes were broadened because her grandmother gladly gave her Nancy Drew books, but also kept her supplied with a variety of other books, better written and of different genres.

Books are especially useful for helping children through difficult situations in their lives: illness, death, abuse, divorce, and so forth. They help open up opportunities for the child to talk about his or her fears and feelings.

Your local librarian can be a good source of information about well-written books appropriate for each age of your grandchildren's lives. Another good source is *The New York Times Parent's Guide to the Best Books for Children* by Eden Ross Lipson. This volume contains summaries of nearly three thousand books for children and young adults, and it indexes them by age appropriateness. One grandmother we know was determined to give her grand-child a collection of award-winning children's books. As she visited bookstores she looked for the familiar gold and silver medallions signifying the book had won the Calde-cott Medal, awarded each year to the best picture book, or the Newberry Award Medal, awarded to the best-written story. Your local Christian bookstore is probably well sup-plied with Bible stories and books that, besides telling a good story, teach values and morals.

Begin early in your grandchildren's lives to take the time to sit and read to them. As they grow, listen to their first stumbling steps at reading on their own. These can be some of the most important and closest times you will spend together. When they are too old for cuddling and being read to, ask them what they are currently reading, then read the same books yourself. It's wonderful when Grandma cares enough to discuss a book knowledgeably, and it gives you yet another way to stay in contact with your grandchildren's thoughts and feelings.

Some of you may be saying, "But you don't know my grandchildren. They aren't readers." Don't be too quick to mark books off your gift list. Whatever your grandchil-dren are interested in, there are books available on that subject. See if you can't find a book so interesting the kids will really want to read it. Just make sure the reading level isn't too high for them to enjoy. If it's too hard, it will discourage them all the more.

## Clothes

Teenagers often say clothes are their favorite presents. The problem is that their ideas of what is great to wear may be miles away from your ideas.

This is not the time to try to force your taste in clothes

on the kids. "Even my six- and eight-year-old grandchildren have darling clothes I have given them that they refuse to wear," Betty said. Ask your grandchildren—not your children—exactly what you should buy for them. Ask them to be specific; brand names are often very important. Searching out cheaper look-alikes is often a waste of both time and money. If you can't afford the retail prices, either look in off-price discount stores or the ever-growing outlet-mall stores for brand names at a discount. If you still can't find their favorite brand or style, consider giving them money to use on clothes they like.

If you are a grandma with a talent for sewing, your grandchildren are especially fortunate. "My grandma was an excellent seamstress," Betty said. "She could copy many of the latest styles for me during my important teenage years when I just had to have that special skirt, blouse, or dress." Today, major pattern companies manufacture patterns for famous designers, so copying styles is much easier.

If you knit or crochet, you can make wonderful gifts that will long be treasured, from baby's first bonnets and booties to sweaters for any age boy or girl.

## Creative Gifts

One woman told us her daughter received a beautiful handmade quilt from her grandmother for a wedding gift. "It's the loveliest thing in her apartment, and she is so proud to show it off!"

Another lady told of her nephew receiving a hand-crocheted tablecloth from his grandmother as a high school graduation gift. "I dreaded watching him open it," she said. "I mean, how much is an eighteen-year-old boy going to care about a crocheted tablecloth? I figured he would open it and say, 'Yep, that's from my grandma. She gave me a tablecloth.' Well, that boy got CDs, money, a television set—all the things a kid his age wants, but the thing he loved the most was Grandma's tablecloth. He walked around all day hugging it, and whenever his buddies came by, he rushed to show them Grandma's gift. How it blessed her heart!''

Gifts that have been especially made by Grandma will be treasured, kept, and remembered through the years. These are the gifts that will be passed on to become the family heirlooms of future generations. We have a good friend who is so talented at making special things for her grandchildren; she even weaves beautiful blankets for them. What special treasures they will be for grandchildren to pass down!

Sometimes we need to take a realistic look at our schedules and do things that are less time-consuming than handmade quilts and tablecloths, yet are just as meaningful to our grandchildren. Because Jan so values the quilts her mother made for her, she has always wanted to make a quilt for her granddaughters. "I really want to and I really mean to, but I never quite get it done," she said. "But I think I have found a solution. I found a quilting place that will do the actual quilting if I sew the pieces of material together."

If you are not that handy and creative but would like to foster creativity in your grandchild, you might visit an art or crafts store and ask the clerk for suggestions about simple projects appropriate for someone your grandchild's age. Or look through your garage and closets and gather old bits of ribbon, boxes, tape, glue, construction paper, paints, crayons, felt-tip markers, and scissors. Put them together with lots of paper and watch as your grandchildren create their own masterpieces.

One of Jan's and her granddaughter's favorite projects is to make place cards for any special family dinner. "I let Michelle pick out the paper, cut it to the size she wants, choose the marker colors, and decide how she wants to decorate the place cards," Jan said. "If it's a birthday dinner, she makes that person a really special one. When it's time for dinner, Michelle is able to proudly set the table with her handmade place cards."

Our friend, author and speaker Lee Ezell, told us about a special project she enjoyed with her grandchildren. She purchased a kit to make a lifelike plaster casting of a child's hand. She helped each of her grandchildren place their little hands in the wet plaster. She told us once the mold was made, filled, and dried, we wouldn't believe the excitement these little ones expressed. What a wonderful gift it made for their parents that Christmas. Children feel a special joy when they can give gifts they make themselves.

Last fall, T-shirt painting was popular. When Betty and her daughter tried it, Betty's grandson and granddaughter stood by fascinated and begging to help. Not wanting to trust the children's artistic ability on Mama's and Grandma's projects, Betty decided to buy inexpensive T-shirts and paints and let them do their own. Together they copied simple designs from a coloring book onto the shirts, and the children had a wonderful time creating. They were so proud of their new shirts they wore them around the neighborhood to show them off. When you are working on projects with your grandchildren, remember that the important thing is to encourage their efforts. Be careful not to demand perfection or finesse.

You can also encourage artistic talents in your grandchildren by giving them gifts of water-based poster paints, watercolors, crayons, markers, finger paints, colored chalk, and end rolls of newsprint. Paintbrushes of different widths, sponges, cotton-tip swabs, a plastic drop cloth, and an apron or smock to protect their clothing will complete their equipment needs. If you prefer, you can make your own finger paint. It's easy. Just combine dry wallpaper paste with warm water, and add food coloring or Tempra® paint for color. Stir the water and color into the paste until it is well mixed and the right consistency, and you are set. (Be sure to clear your refrigerator door. You will want plenty of room to display the masterpieces! A light coat of hairspray will protect pictures drawn with chalk.)

Another economical and fun project is to make your own Play-Doh®. Combine two cups flour, one cup salt, two cups water, and four teaspoons cream of tartar. Add food coloring if you want. Cook the mixture until it comes away from the edge of the pan. (You can knead out any lumps.) Be sure to let it cool before little hands touch it. A rolling pin, cookie cutters, molds, and plastic knives and forks make good tools for working with the Play-Doh®. If you store it tightly covered, it will be ready for another play session.

Is cleanup a problem? It is easier if you have a caddy for storing the supplies. In fact, a plastic caddy filled with art supplies and monogrammed with the child's name in permanent marker makes an excellent gift.

Holidays play an important role in our lives. It's hard to put aside our own desires and concentrate on searching out what is best for our grandchildren at each stage of their lives. But understanding that we are investing in their happy memories makes it well worth the effort.

# Chapter 11

### ❧

# *The Gift of Time and Money*

"Hurry up! You'll make me late!"

"No, I don't have time to do that now. Maybe next week."

"I can't afford that! Do you think I'm made of money?"

Time and money, the twin pressures of today's society. They have always been problems, but it seems these pressures are increasing with every generation. As the cost of living soars ever higher, more and more mothers are forced to join the work force just to make ends meet.

It used to be that grandmothers could always be counted on to baby-sit, to play with the kids, to cook and bake, and to listen to the grandchildren. They were homemakers with no children at home. What else did they have to do with their time?

Author and speaker Patsy Clairmont shared the following poem with us. We wish we could give acknowledgment to the author for the sentiment so well expressed, but she is unknown.

> In the dim and distant past,
> When life's tempo wasn't fast,
> Grandma used to rock and knit,

Crochet, tat and babysit.
When the kids were in a jam,
They could always count on Gram.
In an age of gracious living,
Grandma was the gal for giving.

Grandma now is in the gym,
Exercising to keep slim.
She's off touring with the bunch,
Taking clients out to lunch,
Driving north to ski or curl.
All her days are in a whirl.
Nothing seems to stop or block her,
Now that Grandma's off her rocker!

We don't know about you, but personally we are glad to be off our rockers! Yet there's no doubt that the change in grandmothers' lifestyles has made a profound change in the extended family.

### Life in a Pressure Cooker

"When I was a little girl, my grandparents lived with us," Betty recalled. "Grandma loved to cook. Her fantastic dishes were never-fail. Well, most of the time, anyway. I'll never forget the year we gathered apples and spent hours and hours peeling and slicing them. Some went into pies, but others were destined to become homemade apple-sauce. Grandma hauled out her huge pressure cooker, that intimidating pot with the funny dial on top.

"It was late in the afternoon when the apples went into the pressure cooker. The kitchen was a mess, with apple peelings, cores, sugar, and flour everywhere. The men would soon be home for dinner, and no one had even started to think of what we would eat. We were all tired and hot and the pressure was building. All of a sudden the pressure cooker exploded like a bomb. Applesauce was everywhere—on the walls, on the floor, even dripping off the ceiling. For a moment we stood there stunned. Then Grandma shooed us kids out of the midst of the hot applesauce and bravely grabbed the pot and released the pressure.

"Now we really had a mess on our hands. Not only was there all the cleanup from before, but now the ceiling and floor and cabinets all had to be washed down. We kids cowered in the corner, waiting for the second explosion—Mom. The explosion came, all right, but it wasn't what we expected. It was an explosion of laughter from Grandma! And as the rest of us looked around at the hopelessness of the situation, we all started laughing too."

Many of our lives today are like Grandma's pressure cooker. There isn't enough time for all we have to do. There isn't enough money to go around. Demands, expectations, and obligations press in from all sides. The pressure builds and keeps on building until the pot finally explodes. And it's usually the ones we love the most who end up covered with the mess that spews out.

Sometimes grandmothers can see the pressure building and get there in time to vent the pot and prevent the explosion. Other times we only arrive in time to view the mess. The important thing to realize is that we have a choice. Do we add to the pressure by our recriminations, lectures, or blame-placing? Or do we actively work to relieve the pressure—or if we are too late for that, help clean up the mess? Is our attitude one of hopelessness and helplessness? Can we look at the situation and accept it for what it is, then get in and salvage what we can? We grandmothers can be the catalysts that provide relief for the incredible pressures of time and money that plague families today. It

is a matter of our choosing to take the time and effort to do
so.

## Time Priorities

Arvella Schuller, wife of Dr. Robert Schuller of the Crystal Cathedral, is a prime example of a woman who chooses to make her grandchildren a priority in her life. Mrs. Schuller produces the "Hour of Power" television program, selecting all the music and musicians for the program each week and personally viewing and editing the program. She works with her husband as he prepares his sermons. She handles all the family's personal finances, runs her own household, exercises faithfully, and is on the board and speaks for the American Cancer Society and Hope College, all in addition to being involved in women's ministries at the Crystal Cathedral.

Arvella is also very much involved with each of her five children and their families. Despite her busy schedule and time pressures, Arvella's fifteen grandchildren are a top priority for her. She schedules time to give undivided attention to each child. It may be a lunch or a shopping date. It may be a day, an evening, or a weekend to baby-sit. And whatever the demands on her week, if a grandchild has a special need, Arvella will be there to fill it.

Family has been, and still is, the top priority in Arvella's life. We are convinced the real success of the Schullers is that they are a close family who all love and serve the Lord. Many families in positions of ministry have done wonderful works for God, but at the expense of their own families. Robert and Arvella Schuller made a choice many years ago that they would make their family their first priority, and it shows today.

Some of us didn't always put our own children ahead of

the other priorities in our lives. The wonderful thing about being a grandmother is that it gives us a second chance to order our priorities.

Again and again the two of us have asked ourselves, "How can we write a book on grandparenting when we are so busy grandparenting?" It seemed that whenever we planned to sit down and write, there was a crisis or a time when one grandma or the other really was needed, or a great opportunity came up to enjoy the grandkids. We were so busy putting our theories into practice that we weren't able to get them down on paper. Believe me, we know all about time pressure!

I don't have to tell you that we grandmothers also live in a pressure cooker. But we have the advantage of knowing how fast the years fly by. We understand how really short our time is before the children are grown up and gone. That's why we know the importance of choosing to order our priorities.

One grandmother told about a time when her daughter was having emergency surgery and Grandma was called upon to fill in cooking, cleaning, and caring for her young granddaughter and baby grandson. By the time the house was clean, dinner was prepared, and the kitchen was cleaned up, Daddy arrived to take Grandma home. When little Ashley saw Grandma getting ready to leave, she sank into her little chair and, eyes brimming with tears, looked up at her grandmother and said, "You forgot to play with me, Grandma."

You're a grandmother now! Don't forget to play!

## The Payoff on the Investment of Your Time

A third grader gave the following definition of a grand-mother:

A Grandmother is a lady who has no children of her own. She likes girls. A grandfather is a Man Grandmother. He goes for walks with boys and talks about fishing, tractors, and such.

Grandmothers don't have to do anything except be there. They're old so they shouldn't play hard or run. It is enough if they drive us to the market where the pretend horse is and have plenty of dimes. Or if they take us for walks, they should slow down past things like leaves and caterpillars. Grandmothers never say hurry up!

It is better if they don't typewrite or play cards, except with us. They don't have to be smart, only answer questions like "Why do dogs hate cats?" and "How come God isn't married?"

They don't talk baby talk like visitors do because it is hard to understand. When they read to us, they don't skip or mind if it is the same story again.

Everybody should try to have one, especially if you don't have television, because: GRANDMOTHERS ARE THE ONLY GROWN-UPS WHO HAVE GOT TIME!

Are you willing to invest time to be with your grandchildren? You'll find the payoff is fantastic!

## Material Priorities

"I make money the old-fashioned way. I butter up Grandma!" No, this wasn't spoken by your grandchild. It was a little fellow in a cartoon strip. But it sure strikes a familiar chord in some of us. Because we love our grandchildren, we want to give to them.

When Betty was growing up, she was lucky enough to live within walking distance of both her grandmothers. Grandma Ikey had eight children, eighteen grandchildren, and many great-grandchildren. She also had no extra money. Grandmother Heacock had only two children and five grandchildren. She had plenty of money and she loved to spend it on her grandchildren. But Grandmother Heacock was careful not to let her spending and giving overshadow Grandmother Ikey. Both accepted the fact that they loved their grandchildren dearly, even though each expressed her love differently. "One was able to do more for me materially and could give me more time," Betty said, "yet both had a profound impact on my life."

Betty's more well-to-do grandmother loved to shop. Every Friday, the major department store in their town had a "Friday Surprise" sale. No one knew what would be on sale or what the prices would be until they got there. Every Friday at 9:30 A.M. Grandma Heacock would be waiting for the doors to open. And how she loved to show off the bargains she got! Many were for her grandchildren, but they didn't get those gifts every week. The surprises were put in Grandma's "gift closet," that special, off-limits cupboard where she stored her treasures. On special occasions, or sometimes just because a child needed cheering up, Grandma would dig around in her gift closet and find just the right gift.

As the children grew, the gifts changed. Grandma Heacock's grandchildren could tell by the carefully chosen gifts she gave them that she knew each one well and was thinking of them individually.

"I appreciated Grandma's gifts even more as I grew older," Betty recalls. "When Fred and I were first married, Fred was in school and our income was very limited. Grandma and Grandpa would stop by to take us out to dinner or invite us to their house for a meal. Sometimes they would drop by with a few extra groceries or slip us a little spending money. They took us on vacations, telling us how kind we were to go along and do the driving. They paid the bills, we saw the country, and they thanked us!"

Each gift was freely given. There were no strings attached. Never was there the feeling that a grandchild was obligated to please them in return. The whole attitude was one of celebration of Grandma's love for her grandchildren.

You don't have to be well off to give to your grandchildren. Betty tells how her grandparents went through all their loose change at the end of each day. Every coin that was minted in the year of a great-grandchild's birth was carefully set aside. When the amount reached one hundred dollars, they gave it to the child's parents to invest for the child. "Over the years those investments grew and were added to," Betty said. "The money allowed our children to help pay for their college educations." Those nickels, dimes, and pennies can really add up!

A grandmother who had fallen on tough times had absolutely no money for her grandchildren for Christmas. She dressed up in a Santa outfit and hid in a big box for all the grandchildren to unwrap. When they took off the lid, Grandma popped out with little notes pinned all over her, one for each grandchild: "Jason, I will take you to your softball game every Tuesday." "Marguerite, I will baby-sit you on Friday nights." "Susan, I will take you to all your piano lessons next year." The kids agreed it was the neatest gift anyone had ever given them. Grandma had nothing to give except her time, but what a gift it was!

Some grandparents have reached a place in life where they are financially able to give generous monetary gifts to their grandchildren. It is always wise to consider each child specifically when we make decisions concerning financial gifts. Some children have shown themselves to be responsible, hard-working, and trustworthy. Others seem to be natural-born con artists. Still others expect grandparents to always be there to bail them out of financial difficulty. We must be very careful that our efforts to help don't end up a hindrance in a child's life.

Let us tell you about Travis, a young man who was the apple of his grandparents' eyes. Their first grandchild, Travis was lavished with love and gifts from the day he was born. He grew up knowing if he couldn't get what he wanted from Mom and Dad, he could get it from Grandpa and Grandma. In fact, they overruled and undermined any restrictions Travis's parents placed on him.

After graduation from high school, Travis drifted from job to job, dropping in and out of college classes, and incurring debts and traffic tickets. When Mom and Dad refused to put up with Travis's irresponsible habits any longer, he simply moved in with Grandpa and Grandma. Grandma was certain that if she talked to him and explained the importance of paying bills and tickets and living within his income, he would grow up and become responsible. As for Travis, he assured Grandma that if she would clear up all his debt and give him a fresh start, he would be a new man.

Grandma believed Travis and paid his bills. But Travis's bad financial habits were so ingrained, and Grandma made it so easy on him, that almost immediately he was back in debt again. Unfortunately, Travis's bad habits continued until his grandparents died and there was no one left who would pay his debts. Travis finally learned financial responsibility—the hard way. When he was in his midthirties, he was forced to declare bankruptcy.

Shelly, on the other hand, was a hard-working young woman who was determined to attend a Christian college out of state. Her parents had a large family and no resources to help with her college education. Shelly had applied for and received a small scholarship and some financial aid, and she was working parttime after school and throughout the summer. Yet when all her assets were gathered together, they were not enough to allow her to attend the college.

Shelly's grandparents were financially able to help their granddaughter, but they flatly refused, insisting the local community college was good enough for her.

Both sets of grandparents—Travis's and Shelly's—would have sworn they were acting out of love. The problem was, neither set considered the individual personality of their grandchild and what was really needed the most in that young person's life. Travis needed his grandpa and grandma to say, "No, you must learn financial responsibility." Shelly needed her grandpa and grandma to not only understand how hard she was working to achieve her goals, but to reward her by helping financially.

## Danger, Watch Out!

Perhaps the greatest danger we grandmothers face is failing to understand the proper way to use our money in relation to our grandchildren. Some of us tend to be over-generous, attempting to buy our grandchildren's love, affection, and attention. Others of us tend to withhold it as a punishment for not pleasing us.

Certainly one of the greatest joys of grandparenting is the ability to give our grandchildren gifts, either material gifts or gifts of time. Every grandmother has something to offer her grandchildren. If we can learn to give, keeping in balance our own tendencies to overdo it or to underdo it, we may hit it right. The important thing is that a grandma gives from her heart.

*Chapter 12*

# The Gift of Support

*O*ur good friend Faye Angus has written a little gift book titled *The Gentle Art of Being There.* In our hurried, selfish lifestyle, she says, most of us have forgotten the importance of just "being there." One of the saddest responses to our survey question, "Did you feel your grandparents understood you?" came from a woman who simply wrote, "They didn't really know me."

It doesn't have to be that way for us grandmothers. We can make a choice to be there for our grandchildren. Some of us have the privilege of living close enough to physically be there for them. For others of us, the being there takes a bit more planning and effort (more about long-distance grandparenting in Chapter 16).

### Times of Crisis

Sometimes the best way to be there for our grandchildren is to care for their parents. When a parent is in trauma, the children are profoundly affected. Sometimes we can't do anything for the little ones except help ease their parents' burden so the emotional backwash doesn't splash all over the children. By supporting and encouraging their parents, we are in effect supporting and encouraging our grandchildren.

A time of trauma is not the time for recriminations or lectures or I-told-you-sos. It's the time for encouragement, for nurturing, for hope. It's the time to protect the children from despair, from blame, from their parents' frustration and anger, from being smothered by the neediness of Mom and Dad.

Betty's daughter Susan went through a painful pregnancy. Her doctor said, "Take it easy," but how could she? Her husband was overseas, and Susan was working full time as well as taking care of her two-year-old daughter. Betty was able to step in and help care for her little granddaughter through her mother's pregnancy—and miscarriage—and Susan's recovery.

It's hard to watch a child go through a tough experience without pouring out advice. Mothers want to fix things, to make everything all right. But unless our grown children ask for our input, we need to discipline ourselves to simply be there, listen, and give whatever support we can to them and to our grandchildren.

Whether our children are just too wrapped up in their own situations to have emotional energy for dealing with their own children, or whether they are the source of their children's frustration, we can make ourselves available as the sounding boards for our grandchildren. We can be there to give them the full attention that is so necessary in times of crisis.

## Minor Crises

Not all crises are as major as illness or divorce or financial disaster. Sometimes it seems like a little thing but it's major to the one who is experiencing it.

A young lady named Ann told us she called her grandmother in a panic because she had to have a choir outfit immediately. "Mother was too busy," Ann said. "She told me I'd just have to do without it." But Ann knew she would simply die if Friday came and she was the only choir member without the proper outfit. Would Grandma please, please make it for her? Now, Grandma knew Ann wouldn't really die without that outfit. But she also could tell how very important it was to Ann to have it. Although Grandma was busy, she readjusted her schedule and got to work on Ann's choir dress.

What Grandma did for Ann was far more important than simply providing her with a new choir outfit. Grandma understood what was important to her. Grandma didn't lecture her on the irresponsibility of waiting until the last minute. She knew Ann's mother had done enough of that for both of them. "But she did call Ann's mother and ask if it was all right to make the dress," Ann said. "And she did remind me with a kiss that I might do it differently next time."

When is it appropriate to step in and rescue our children or grandchildren? That's a tough question to answer. Each grandmother must evaluate her own situation individually. But we have put together a few guidelines to help you think it through:

## 1. Consider the grandchild's temperament.

Is this a child who has a tendency to turn every situation into a crisis? Does the child often overlook personal responsibility and depend on others to take responsibility for him or her? Does he or she take on more than can be humanly handled by one person? Is he or she a procrastinator, always waiting until the last minute to get things done? Does the child have a hard time getting motivated?

If so, ask yourself what you might do to encourage this grandchild in some of these areas. Stepping in may hinder his or her growth and keep the child from a healthy struggle to work it out.

## 2. Consider the home situation.

What is happening at the child's home? Are there stresses and tensions between family members? Are economic pressures putting a strain on the family? Are there personality conflicts among family members? Is there an illness in the family that is demanding all the time and attention of the other members? Are Mom and Dad having marital problems? Do the child's parents have expectations of him or her that are too high or too low? Is the child being misunderstood or used as a family scapegoat? Is the child being treated as an adult while he or she is still a child? Are the child's needs being overlooked because he or she is too good, or too afraid to make his or her needs or wants known? If your answers to these questions show your grandchild is in a difficult home situation, you will need to consider intervening.

## 3. Be aware of any power struggles that are going on between your grandchild and his or her parents.

When every situation is turned into a win-or-lose battle, nothing anyone does is going to help. In the end, no one wins and everyone loses. In an article titled "When Kids Drive you Crazy," published in the March 1992 issue of *Focus on the Family* magazine, Dr. James Dobson put it this way: "It will come as no surprise to parents (or grandparents) I am sure, that children can be quite gifted at power games. These contests begin in earnest when children are between twelve and fifteen months of age."

## Power Games

Children aren't the only ones who play power games. Many parents are also guilty. Even grandmothers can get in on the act. Whenever the issue at hand is not really the true issue, but is just a smoke screen to cover up a win-or-lose contest, the best thing a grandmother can do is withdraw. Your goal is to evaluate what is happening in the situation and to determine how, if at all, you can be of help.

Power struggles within families rely on a "top-dog-versus-underdog" mentality. Someone must always get the best of someone else. The same people don't always play the same role, however. The power may shift. If a wife is constantly the underdog in power struggles with her husband, for instance, she may make sure that in relationships with at least one of her children, she is top dog. The poor underdog child, on the other hand, may be determined to be top dog with a sibling or with other kids in the neighborhood or at school. The father's top-dog act at home may even be the result of feeling like an underdog at work. Or it may carry over from the days when he was at the bottom of the heap as a young boy.

Are you facing a power struggle? Here are three points that may help you correctly evaluate what you're up against.

## 1. Is this an issue of false pride?

Pride issues often stem from low self-esteem. People who are unsure of their own value and worth may try to bluff their way through life by being bullies, forcefully overpowering everyone around them. Or, in an effort to win sympathy and recognition for themselves, they may choose to become permanent underdogs or martyrs. Both extremes stem from not being able to recognize one's own personal worth. Many teenagers are masters at using both extremes to win. If they come out on top, they overpower and get their way. But if they are overpowered, they still win because then they can tell the world about their cruel, hard-hearted parents or grandparents who just do not understand.

"Our oldest daughter, Tara, and I played this power-struggle game almost from the moment she was born," Betty admits. "I wasn't at all sure of myself as a new mother, and I'm certain that from the moment of her birth she sensed my insecurity. From her earliest days, if I said yes, she said no. If I said no, she said yes. Our relationship was one continual argument, a daily power struggle to see which one of us would win each battle. More often than not, the issue was unimportant, but to me it was 'the principle of the thing.' I realize now that 'the principle' I was fighting for was my right to win!"

The struggle for control continued into Tara's marriage. "Only thing was, she married someone who struggled with her as much as I did," Betty said. "He wanted to be in control of her, and I wanted to be in control of her. So now instead of both of us battling her, we began to battle each other to get her to do what we wanted. For instance, he wouldn't let her come to see us without his coming along. It was unthinkable to me that we should have to have him all the time and that she should have to ask his permission for everything she did, and I told her so."

It took a crisis to settle the conflict. Betty took her other two daughters to Texas to celebrate Tara's thirtieth birthday. "We had all these plans," Betty recalls. "We took care of the children so she and her husband could go out of town the night before, then he was to bring her back to her surprise party. We totally cleaned the house from top to bottom. We hung balloons and banners, and bought a lovely cake."

But when Tara got home, she didn't seem to notice all the work the three had done. The strokes and gushing appreciation Betty had expected weren't there. Instead there was too much nit-picking about things that weren't done right—a painting was framed wrong, a shelf hung in the wrong place. "The real problem was that Tara was afraid her husband would be unhappy with what we'd done," Betty relates. Tara was stressed and feeling torn, and Betty was feeling angry, used, and unappreciated. Then and there, Betty decided she wouldn't come to Texas again.

But this time something different happened. This time Tara's husband, Mike, took Betty into the garage, closed the door behind them, and talked to her. "We love you," he said firmly, "but this is how things have to be."

It was a very, very painful time for Betty. She went home and wrote a letter to her daughter, expressing all the things she was feeling. Tara took the letter and cut it apart. She answered each piece and sent it back. For the first time, mother and daughter were beginning to let each other know their deep feelings, fears, and concerns. "It was a terribly difficult growth process for all of us," Betty said. "But out of it came a real love for my son-in-law. Once we were able to get through the top-dog–underdog battle, we developed a great relationship." Today Betty feels a freedom for Tara to be her own person who is not under her mother's control. "But," Betty said, "it has been a process."

It is vital that we recognize the need to make changes in ourselves. Note the word *ourselves*. We cannot change the people around us; we can only change ourselves. Growing and adapting and refining ourselves is a never-ending process.

If we can remove our pride from the old power struggles, we can see more clearly the issue at hand. Then everyone involved is free to make suggestions on how to solve the real problem without keeping score.

## 2. Are there secondary issues that need to be resolved?

How many times have you gotten up in the morning feeling out of sorts, grumpy, maybe slightly depressed? Notice how on such mornings it drives you absolutely crazy when your husband leaves an uncapped toothpaste tube on the bathroom counter, or your grandchild eats with her fingers and feeds the dog from her plate? Pushed over the edge, right? Now, it may be perfectly true that your husband needs to learn to put the cap back on the toothpaste and that your grandchild could use some table manners. But an out-of-control outburst at this time only serves to set off a power struggle.

When Betty's daughter and her family were in town for a week recently, Betty watched the interaction between Tara and her own little daughter Toria. It was like watching an instant replay of herself twenty-five years earlier. Later, when Betty and Tara talked about it, Tara asked, "Does it make you happy to see me getting paid back?"

"No," Betty answered honestly. "It grieves me to watch it and remember how much we argued. It hurts to realize I was responding to you on a childish level rather than acting like the adult I was supposed to be. I wish I had known then what I know now."

"But, Mom," Tara pressed, "how can I stop without letting her have the last word?"

Reflecting back, Betty knew that had been her problem

exactly. As a young mother she hadn't been about to let Tara have the last word. Certainly she had loved her daughter dearly, and she really wanted to raise her properly. She had wanted Tara to learn responsibility, to be able to pitch in and get the job done. But those were secondary issues. The real conflict had centered around who was going to be top dog and who was going to be underdog.

Betty gently explained to Tara the evidence of the power struggle that lay beneath each conflict.

"But how do I train my children or teach them responsibility?" Tara asked. "I want to be more than just a passive mother."

Good question, Tara. And it leads us directly to question number three.

### 3. How can I remove the urgency illusion?

We all have the tendency to think if we don't get this situation under control right this very minute, we will lose control forever. But a lifetime of involvement in win-or-lose power struggles is not going be overturned in a moment. It takes time to learn to eliminate issues of pride and poor self-concept, and to recognize and deal with secondary causes such as emotional reactions and the desire to get a job done. And it takes time to teach a child responsibility. Some days we will do well. Other days—well, we all experience our share of those *other* days.

If we can recognize the times when we have allowed the win-or-lose game to get the upper hand, we will be well on our way to being able to overcome its control over us. And being willing to go back and acknowledge to your child or grandchild that your attitude was wrong in a specific situation can help set that child free from the control of the win-or-lose cycle.

Perhaps only now, as a grandparent, do you recognize and understand the mistakes you made as a parent. The good news is that it's still not too late to change. And if you do change, you will be giving your grandchild a wonderful example to follow.

# Chapter 13

*&*

# *The Gift of Wisdom*

*A* young newlywed named Donna responded to our survey questionnaire. While her husband, Jim, was undergoing basic training in the navy, Donna was staying with her parents. One morning Jim called Donna. He was terribly lonely, he said, and had arranged for her to come and live where he was stationed, even though they could only see each other on weekends. Donna was excited, but her mother was upset. "Jim's asking too much," she argued. "You'll be in a strange town, away from your family and friends. And you'll be alone all week. You should stay with us until Jim's basic training is over."

It so happened that Donna's grandmother overheard the entire exchange and watched as Donna ran off in tears. Grandma waited a few minutes and then followed her. She put her arms around her granddaughter, hugged her close, and said, "Donna, your place is with your husband. Your mother isn't thinking of your marriage. She's only thinking of herself."

"My grandmother's willingness to step in and help me sort through the situation was a real gift," Donna told us. "Her action helped me make the right decision."

Did Donna's grandmother do the right thing? As grandparents we find ourselves seeing situations from a different perspective than we did when we were just parents. Sometimes our reactions are almost totally opposite from what they would have been back then. As young mothers, many of our decisions were based on the question "What will people think?" Now, mellowed by time and distance, we have learned to ask instead, "What is best for this child?" No longer having to be "perfect mothers," we can afford to ease up on our expectations.

Yet most of us have to face the question "When should I give them the benefit of my wisdom and when should I leave them alone and let my children (or grandchildren) make their own mistakes?" There is the danger of not acting when we should, the danger of acting too quickly, and the danger of acting with the wrong motives. Perhaps true wisdom is found in the ability to discern between control for control's sake—that is, stepping in and giving advice in order to get your way—and seeing what is most needed for the good of everyone involved.

## Grandparenting Styles Make a Difference

In situations that require wisdom and action, we all need to ask ourselves, "How am I likely to react? What do I need to guard against? What do I need to push myself to do?" To some degree this will be influenced by your style of grandmothering.

If you are a doer grandmother, you may tend to be too quick to act. You need to pause, step back for a minute, and make sure you understand the situation before you do anything. And take care to temper your actions with tenderness.

If you are a dreamer grandmother, you will be quick to feel your grandchild's pain, just as Donna's grandmother was. But realize that you can be so sensitive to everyone you won't do anything at all. Be willing to champion your grandchild if it is called for.

If you are a discoverer, your inclination may be to say, "Well, this is what needs to be done, but he or she is old enough to know it, so I won't say anything." You, too, need to be willing to get involved and act.

If you are a director, you will be quick to look at the *shoulds*. Without looking at both sides, you may be tempted to say something like, "You are the child, so you should do what your mother says." You will need to listen to both sides, put away the rule book, and temper your action with evidence that you care.

Wisdom is being able to look at your own style, to look at the people involved, and to act carefully. The important thing is to resist the temptation to base your decision merely on your own reactions and, instead, to look at the bigger picture. You may need to draw upon the character-istics of other grandmothering styles. Great! You're not stuck with your style and natural response in every situa-tion. It's up to you to choose your response according to what's needed by that person at that time.

Because the style of grandmothering differs so greatly between the two of us, we can understand the difficulties here. This question of Donna's grandmother's involve-ment is a good way to show both ways we would be most likely to respond.

Dreamer Jan's opinion is, "Grandma was right to step in, but she should have been more sensitive about Donna's mother."

In contrast, doer Betty's opinion is, "I can't believe there's even a question. Grandmothers should be willing to do more." The best course is somewhere between the two of us. We can see the negative in each other's opinion, but we can also see the positive—and can learn from that.

"Had it not been for Jan's sensitivity and her depth of compassion and feeling, I hate to think of how I would blunder through my 'just doing things' without considering the feelings of others," said Betty.

"Without Betty to push me and encourage me to take action when it is needed, I would have thought and felt and empathized forever and never have done anything," said Jan.

As we have worked together to sharpen our grandparenting skills, and as we have prayed over our concerns, failures, and excitement, we have both gained the ability to step back and look at the bigger picture. We are a doer and a dreamer who, together, have learned to be focused.

## *Wisdom Is . . .*

What is wisdom, and how does it relate to grandparenting? According to the dictionary, wisdom is "accumulated knowledge or learning, good sense, a wise attitude or course of action." As grandmothers, we have had more time to accumulate knowledge and figure out what works and what doesn't. But that's not enough to make us wise. We also need the good sense to know the importance of having the right attitude before we embark on a course of action. And we need to consider timing and the ability to know the difference between helping and interfering.

### Look for Patterns

When a situation occurs over and over again without being resolved, it may be an appropriate time to intervene. It is especially important when a child's self-esteem is being damaged. Emotional, verbal, or physical abuse may be occurring without the parents' awareness. This can happen, even when the particular problem seems minor.

Betty recalls her daughter arguing with her young son over the clothes he had chosen to wear. Timmy, a strong-willed two-year-old, insisted on picking out his own clothes, but the combination he had chosen didn't go together at all. Mommy said, "Absolutely not!" and a royal battle began. This scene was repeated daily for weeks.

Timidly Betty asked her daughter, "Why does it matter so much if his clothes match? He'll only be playing around home."

"My son is not going to be seen wearing clothes that don't match," her daughter insisted. It was a matter of Mommy's pride.

Now, Betty's feeling was that little Timmy had reasons for his choice in clothes: they were comfortable and he liked them. He didn't understand the rules of conformity. In his mind, they looked just fine.

"My mind went back to Tara's childhood and the sweater and pants she wore almost daily for six months," Betty said. "The pants were threadbare and halfway up her legs. The sweater was so small her tummy was bare most of the time. But it was her favorite outfit. Yes, it hurt my pride to have people see her dressed that way. And she's embarrassed, too, when she sees the pictures from that year. But at that time it was very important to her to be in charge of what she wore."

Betty asked her to reconsider her insistence that Timmy dress to please her, gently reminding Tara of her own feelings as a child. They talked together about times when it was important that his clothes match and times when it really didn't matter. Having made her point, Betty dropped the subject and left the decision up to her daughter.

Jan realizes there are many times she jumped in with "helpful" advice when she should have waited before speaking up. "I try hard to be sensitive to a situation, especially since I am the mother of boys so I am always going be the mother-in-law to my grandchildren's mothers," she said. "Yet I know I can get intrusive with my not-so-subtle 'help.' The other day I realized it was the third or fourth time I had asked about my youngest granddaughter's diaper rash and had made suggestions to her mother. Once would have been entirely enough. My gift of wisdom could have been to let my granddaughter's mom do what she felt was best and wait for her to ask my advice if she wanted it."

Timing is so important. There is a time to speak up and there is a time to keep your mouth shut. A wise grandma will be aware of the difference.

## Timing

*When* we share is often more important than *what* we share. By nature, some of us tend to be reactors. Something happens, and we react—too often with responses that are not well thought out. What we say or how we say it may lead other people to feel they are being personally attacked. This puts them on the defensive, and they instinctively strike back. The result is that all helpful communication is lost, and we become adversaries.

Except in cases of physical danger, it is better to allow some time to elapse between seeing a situation you feel you need to discuss and actually discussing it. We find it helpful to ask ourselves questions that help clarify what we are feeling: *What is this triggering in me that is causing me to react this way? What is going on inside me that makes me react so immediately?*

As Betty watched the interaction between her daughter and her grandson over his choice of clothes, she asked herself, *Why is this bothering me so much?* She realized it was because of her own dependence as a young mother on what other people had thought. She had transmitted that value to her daughter, who was in the process of passing it on to yet another generation. These *Why?* questions help us check our motives.

When you feel confident you have uncovered your reasons for sharing your thoughts and observations, and when you have determined that what's happening isn't just a one-time thing but a pattern, start watching for an appropriate time to share your feelings.

Look for a time when the parent is alone with you. Don't put him or her on the defensive by staging a confrontation in front of others. Choose a time when he or she is somewhat relaxed and can listen to what you have to say.

When the time is right, state your observations clearly as your own personal opinion. Be careful not to attack, blame, or accuse. Keep your voice even and calm. Asking questions may help you understand the other person's point of view. If the parent takes offense, try not to argue or become defensive. Simply state the problem as you see it and offer some possible suggestions. Don't demand immediate changes. Allow him or her the freedom to think about what you have said and to take responsibility for finding the best solutions.

While visiting her daughter's family, a grandmother named Joan noticed that her son-in-law, Mark, was very critical of his thirteen-year-old daughter, Brianna. He criticized her clothes, her hairdo, and how long she spent in the bathroom getting ready every day. He was impatient with her long telephone calls and her messy room.

The family had just moved, and although Brianna badly wanted to be liked and accepted, she had not yet found her place of comfort among friends.

One morning, upon discovering that Brianna had once again left her curling iron turned on, Mark exploded. That evening, after reciting her list of faults, he told his daughter she could not use the curling iron for two weeks. Brianna burst into tears and ran into her room, slamming the door behind her.

Grandma understood how devastating the loss of a curling iron could be to an insecure teenager. So later that evening, after Mark had calmed down and Brianna was in bed, Grandma asked Mark if she could talk to him. Gently she explained teenage girls' feelings. Then, expressing her opinion that Mark's punishment was perhaps too severe, she suggested that he reconsider and look for another way to help Brianna overcome her irresponsibility. Having stated her case, Grandma went on to bed, leaving Mark to make his own decision.

Grandma Joan was a wise grandmother.

## Not Interfering

As our children begin to have children, we quickly become aware of how greatly the theories of child rearing can vary from generation to generation. Many mothers of today are highly educated and well versed in the latest psychological trends. They go through their pregnancies attending prenatal classes, carefully watching everything they eat or drink, and studying every book and article on raising children. When they bring that precious little bundle home, they have every intention of being the perfect parents for the perfect child. We who have already raised our children remember our similar hopes and dreams.

With our wisdom of hindsight, we are sometimes tempted to immediately deflate the dreams of those starry-eyed new parents. It is helpful at those times of temptation to remember how we resented the ones who tried to direct our lives.

Every grandmother has at one time or another watched her grandchildren's parents do something that caused her heart to cringe. How we want to spare our children and grandchildren the pain that results from the mistakes we see being made!

Betty lives near a neighborhood recreation area where many kids play team sports. As she and her husband, Fred, watch the interactions between child players and their parents, their hearts ache to see so many little spirits being crushed by overly competitive parents.

One day a darling little boy of about seven ran past them, all decked out in his miniature basketball uniform.

"Do you like playing basketball?" Fred asked.

"Not really," the little fellow replied. "I can never play good enough for my daddy."

As they watched the boy that day, they understood what he meant. When the starting lineup was chosen and the little guy wasn't included, he sat down on the bench without complaint. But his father started yelling at him, "Tell the coach you should start! You're the best!"

When he did get to play, his parents were overruling the coach's commands on every play and position. The coach would say, "Stand here," or "Guard that person," and his father would yell, "Get the ball!" or "Shoot!" The poor child didn't know who to listen to. When the game was over, Daddy insisted it was the coach's fault the boy's team lost. "He didn't use you enough," the dad said. But it was obvious from the dejected look in the little boy's eyes he carried the weight personally of being "trashed" by the other team.

Could this boy's grandparents have intervened without interfering? Possibly. If their relationship with his parents was a healthy one, if they had been careful to maintain open communication, if they had consistently treated each other with respect, it would certainly have helped to discuss the issue. Although it would be up to the parents to change or persist in their pressure on the boy, whatever happened, the grandparents would know they tried.

When you do present your views, lay them out simply and clearly. Point out what you have observed and the impact such actions or words may carry, then let the matter drop. You have done your part. Now it is up to the parent to decide whether your point is valid and calls for specific action.

The time to tell the child's parents what to do is when the parents ask you. Otherwise, suggest other ways they might handle the situation, but always leave Mom and Dad the freedom to handle it in their own way.


## *Letting Go*

Perhaps the hardest part of our grandmothering job description is letting go. We can see so clearly the long-term results of choices, actions, and reactions, of both our grandchildren and their parents. We want so badly to protect them all from doing the same stupid things we did. *I could fix that problem,* we tell ourselves. But it's an unfortunate fact of human nature that often the only way people learn is the hard way. Will our children and grandchildren learn vicariously through our experiences, or will they have to make their own mistakes? The choice is theirs.

A grandmother wrote to tell us the sad story of her daughter, Paula, her son-in-law, Tony, and their baby, little Tony. Tony and Paula had a very unstable marriage. Tony had been reared in an abusive family, and when things didn't go well, he did what his father had done—turned his anger on his wife and son. Paula's parents were extremely concerned about Paula and their grandson. Several times neighbors called to complain about the way Tony was treating them.

One day Paula asked her parents if they would take care of little Tony. Grandma and Grandpa readily said, "Yes!" As they cleaned up the dirty, neglected little boy, they noticed he had bruises and abrasions all over his body. Although they were torn between love and loyalty to their daughter and their love and concern for little Tony, they finally called the Department of Social Services. Little Tony was awarded to them on a finding of parental neglect.

After little Tony had lived with his grandparents for over a year, Paula and Tony, armed with proof of a job and a new apartment, petitioned the court for his return. They were granted custody. In less than two months, Grandma and Grandpa got a telephone call from the hospital emergency room saying little Tony had a head injury from being hit by his father. Would they please come and get the boy?

Little Tony's grandparents are now petitioning the court for permanent custody of their grandson.

Wisdom doesn't imply that any of us has all the answers. We have many opinions, and we have reasons why we believe our opinions are valid. But our children may have different values and opinions, and we need to recognize and respect their rights to view things differently than we do. Yet sometimes, with some parents, someone has to step in and say, "Enough is enough."

What is wisdom? It is understanding we don't have all the answers. It is accepting that some of our answers may not be acceptable to our children. It is knowing that when we raised our children, we did the best we could with what we knew and who we were at the time. It is trusting that our children will do the best they can with what they know and who they are now. It is believing that God loves and cares for our grandchildren even more than we do. Ultimately, true wisdom is learning to release our grandchildren into God's loving care.

# Chapter 14

# The Gift of Sharing God

*J*esus wuves me, dis I know . . . I got de joy, joy, joy, joy down in my 'eart, down in my 'eart . . . Jesus wuves de 'ittle chilwen, all de chilwen of de worl' . . ."

As Betty listened to her little two-year-old granddaughter happily playing and singing a medley of songs in the background, joyful memories flooded her thoughts: her own grandmother working in the kitchen while little Betty played happily and sang those very same songs, songs her own grandma had sung to her.

"I stopped to think about Grandma and how she shared her love of God with me," Betty said. "Grandma didn't have much education, and she knew nothing about theology, but she sure knew how to love. For more than fifty years she taught Sunday school to two-year-olds."

Betty recalled how those simple songs sounded on the old pump organ in the church basement. She remembered how every Saturday her grandparents would go over to the church to make sure the Sunday school room was ready for the children. All the fresh juice and animal crackers Grandma served. The special little things she always had ready to illustrate the Bible story—construction-paper flowers with the words "He careth for you" carefully printed by hand, or small bags of rice to represent the bags of grain Joseph gave his brothers. The flannel boards, the piles of crayons and paper. The open, welcoming arms of Grandma.

"When Grandma died at eighty-five, the church was filled for her funeral," Betty recalls. "Many stood to pay tribute to her living demonstration of God's love in action. A lot of people have personal relationships with God because Grandma loved their little children."

Betty never recalls her grandmother preaching about God. She doesn't remember her judging or condemning others. Those around her saw in her a God who really cared for people, a God to whom each person was important, however small or insignificant that one might be. They saw a God who could be trusted to always be there, ready to welcome each person with open arms. "Hers was a simple faith—childlike, really," Betty said. "Yet I wonder if Grandma, in all her simplicity, wasn't a more effective evangelist than the world's greatest preachers."

## Grandma's Spiritual Guidance

We are both active in women's Bible study groups. Many of the women who attend were not raised with any religious affiliation and have only recently begun attending a church or Bible study. What draws them now to search for answers in the Scriptures? Over and over again we hear the same answer: "I had a grandmother who loved God. She talked to me about Him and she prayed for me."

Most of these women are the children of highly educated, "liberal" parents who, wanting their children to make their own choices concerning religion, never exposed them to any religious training. They grew up feeling spiritually lost and rootless—except for Grandma.

### Share with Love—Even When It's Hard

Simply because of our personalities, there are bound to be some grandchildren we will "take to" more than others. A grandmother we know took her two teenage grandsons out to breakfast. The younger one has really been a better boy in a lot of ways—well behaved, cooperative, never rebellious—yet his grandmother finds him harder to like. Why? Because as a small child he threw frequent temper tantrums—just as his mother had done many years before.

One grandmother told of visiting her little granddaughter and her family. Grandma could soon see the little girl's daddy overlooked her a lot, giving his attention to her younger sister instead. "She does a lot of annoying things to get attention," the grandmother said, "and I found myself also getting annoyed with her. Sometimes I, too, have trouble liking her. But at those times I pause and pray, *Lord, Katy needs my love. Help me give it to her.* By myself, I get impatient and annoyed and want to shape her up. But the Lord gives me an extra abundance of love for her."

If you have a grandchild who's hard to love, tell the Lord about it and ask Him to love that child through you. It may help to visualize yourself as a funnel. If the child rejects the love you offer, understand it's not your love that's being rejected, it's God's love. Ask God to show you one special thing you can accentuate in that child. Choose to focus on the good and the positive. Then ask God to fill you to running over with love.

## *But How Can I Share My Love of God?*

Learning a short Scripture verse became such an interesting game between Jan and her granddaughter that every time Michelle came over to Grandma's house she asked to play it. "We used to set up little rewards like making popcorn and seeing if we could learn a phrase before helping ourselves to five pieces. Or we would decide that the reward for learning a verse would be to go over to the park and swing for awhile." It's important that learning about God be kept a pleasurable experience.

Sharing God with our grandchildren doesn't require lots of training or systematized steps. In fact, it should be a natural part of our interaction with them. It can start with the simple songs you sing to them as babies. "Jesus Loves Me" is ever so much more comforting than "Rock-a-bye Baby"!

Children take in so much more than we realize. Betty's tiny granddaughter singing those simple songs is evidence of the importance of what we hear. Many wonderful, simple books are available that can help reinforce God's love to children and animals and the world. If we listen carefully to the children's questions and take care to answer with a simple philosophy ("God makes animals too"), we are sharing God with them.

Don't worry that you are not an expert on religion. Just be yourself. If God is important to you, you only have to share your own thoughts and simple experiences. Begin with the practical, accessible people and events of everyday life—meals, school activities, Mom and Dad's occupations, neighbors, relatives, and other ideas. Without forcing it or preaching, look for opportunities to bring God into the child's everyday life.

## Talking and Listening

As you share your own views on God, be sure to encourage your grandchildren to share their views as well. Listen to their questions and don't let their doubts frighten you. Pay close attention so you can hear the unspoken feelings hiding behind the words they say. You may be tempted to "correct" their misconceptions by discounting their experiences or feelings, or reacting with dogmatism. Don't. Instead, seek a balance between sharing your own views and being open and willing to listen to theirs. As you give children attention and respect for what they have to say, you will be earning their respect. In turn, they will be much more likely to appreciate your views.

Mealtime is a wonderful time to share God with your grandchildren in a natural way. You may begin with a simple prayer before the meal. Then you might ask, "Where does our food come from? Can we consider it a gift from God?" You might add, "That's why we thank God for it, and for our parents and grandparents who provide it for us, and for a healthy body that uses the food to let us work and play." At another meal, you might talk about how you enjoy planning and preparing special meals for them because you love them so much. Another time you could tell the story of Moses and the Israelites in the wilderness, and how God provided food and water for them because He loved them. Throughout the Bible, food is used to illustrate how much God loves us and cares about our needs.

A good way to share God's love with your grandchildren is by demonstrating the way His love shows through us as we care about each other's needs. Talk about how much God loves every one of us and wants us to love each other, even when we don't always agree with others or like what they are doing.

Sometimes family gatherings are not happy, and angry words are spoken. Sensitive grandmothers may use these occasions to draw their grandchildren aside, find out their feelings, and help them understand what is happening. It's also a great time to pray with them.

## By Example

One lady told us of the spring break her grandchildren spent at her home. It was Easter time, and in preparation for Good Friday services she had been telling the children the story of Jesus' betrayal and trial. She had particularly emphasized the great love of God, who sent His only Son to die to pay the price for our sins. She also talked about Jesus' love, so great that He even asked God to forgive the people who had betrayed Him and were killing Him.

By the end of the week, the children had tired of the novelty of being at Grandma's house, and Grandma had run out of ideas and patience for entertaining them. Besides, she needed to prepare for the big family dinner they would have when the children's parents arrived. Grandma separated the bickering kids once again and gave them strict instructions not to play in the living room. Then she busied herself in the kitchen.

The next thing Grandma heard was a loud crash. Running to investigate, she found the children in the forbidden living room, Stacy with a nasty bump on her forehead and crying loudly. The end table was overturned beside her, and Grandma's precious antique lamp lay shattered on the floor. In her worry about Stacy and her anger about the disobedience and the broken lamp, Grandma said some very harsh words to the children. As she tended to Stacy's bump and to cleaning up the mess, she let them know in no uncertain terms they were "bad" and the lamp was "ir-replaceable." She sent them to their room to think about their disobedience, then she went back to her dinner preparations.

As she worked, God brought to Grandma's mind the many lessons she had been trying to teach the children that week about God's love and forgiveness. He reminded her that His loss of a Son was much greater than her loss of a lamp. The children hadn't meant to break the lamp, but those who betrayed and killed His Son had done it on purpose. God also reminded her of the many times she had disobeyed God, and how He had patiently forgiven her again and again. Could she do any less for her grandchildren?

Grandmother went up to the bedroom and gathered the children in her arms. Though they wouldn't look her in the eyes, she held them tight and asked them to forgive her for the way she acted and for the words she said. She told them how God had reminded her of the stories she had been telling them all week, and she forgave them for their disobedience and for breaking her lamp. She reminded them that apologizing means more than simply saying, "I'm sorry." It also means trying not to disobey again. Then she explained to the children that even when she was angry at them, she still loved them very, very much. It was their actions she didn't like, not them.

What a wise grandmother! In openly confessing her attitude of anger to her grandchildren, and by telling them of God's tender love and forgiveness, she was able to demonstrate a real-life example of God's love and forgiveness toward us, even though we don't deserve it. An antique lamp for a meaningful lesson on God's love—this grandma insists it was a worthy trade-off. We agree.

### The Questions Will Come

"Our God reigns! Our God reigns!" little Michelle sang over and over. Finally her mother asked her what the words meant. "I guess it means God sends the rain," Michelle said. Jan had taught her granddaughter the song without giving a second thought to the abstract concept of God reigning. Now, older and wiser, Michelle sings the song with understanding.

Even if your grandchildren are being reared in homes where God and religion are not a part of the family conversation, they will hear about God. Other family members, neighbors, friends, television programs, movies, and books often refer to God. Our Pledge of Allegiance and our coins both make reference to God. Biblical stories such as those describing Noah's ark and Jonah and the whale are likely to bring up questions about Him.

At one time or another, most children ask questions about God. By thinking of answers ahead of time, you will be more prepared for the questions when they come. Here are some common questions you might want to be thinking about:

1. Is God a person? Is He a man or a woman?
2. Where does God live?
3. What does God look like?
4. Does God hear me when I pray?
5. Does God answer all my prayers?
6. How can I tell if God is around?
7. Does God know me and love me?
8. Does God love everyone, even bad people?
9. Does God make babies?
10. Why does God let there be wars?

11. Can God do everything?
12. How can God help me?
13. Does God still do miracles?
14. Is my minister, priest, or rabbi always right?
15. How can I know God better?

As you form answers to these questions, focus on what really matters to the children. They don't want a long theological treatise on the subject, just a short, simple answer. It's helpful to rephrase the questions to see if you really understand what the children are asking. If they show more interest in a particular area, help them learn to use a Bible dictionary, a commentary, or a concordance to find more information. If you don't know the answer to a question, tell your grandchildren you don't know. Share with them what you think and why you feel the way you do. Trust yourself to answer well. Trust God to guide you. And trust your grandchild to ask wisely and to understand the answers.

Many children are inhibited about expressing their feelings about God. Encourage them to say whatever they feel or think. Whatever they say, don't shut them off by stating, "You shouldn't believe that." If you feel they may have the wrong concept or image of God, probe deeper for why they feel the way they do. Then seek to lead them to the right concept in a positive manner.

## Enjoy the Experience

Above all, sharing God with your grandchildren should be a positive, uplifting experience for all of you. To do it in a harsh, legalistic, judgmental way will instill fear and guilt in them. And any relationship founded on fear and guilt is doomed to fail. How much healthier it is to teach obedience to God as a response to His love. And it's far more likely to have permanent results.

If you make it a priority to experience God's presence in your life every day, it will naturally follow that He will be meaningful in the lives of your grandchildren.

Betty's grandchildren, from the oldest to the youngest, know Grandma has her devotions first thing in the morning while she is still in bed. When they spend the night, they are in her bed at the crack of dawn. But when Grandma is ready for her devotions, they either get up on their own or lie quietly beside her. Eight-year-old Timmy has recently started asking her to read the Bible aloud. Elizabeth, the two-year-old, now associates Grandma's bed with the Bible. One weekend when Elizabeth was visiting, Betty was worn out and went to her bedroom to catch a quick nap. Elizabeth came running in calling, "No sleep, Grandma, no sleep. Read your Bible."

There are many ways to share God with your grandchildren, but the greatest way of all is through your own example. A motto for a grandmother who loves the Lord is found in Psalm 71:18: "Even when I am old and gray, / do not forsake me, O God, / till I declare your power to the next generation, / your might to all who are to come" (NIV).

The eight gifts we have described in this part of *The Grandmother Book* are the heart of grandparenting. There is great joy, but as in all aspects of life, the flip side is sometimes pain. Part 4 deals with challenges—disciplining our grandchildren and being long-distance grandmothers. One chapter takes a realistic look at some of the pain grandparents experience—the divorce of their children and its effect on those precious grandchildren, or the abuse of a grandchild. Here grandmothers are often called upon to fill in the gap in an entirely different way. Finally, we'll look at the challenge of praying with our grandchildren.

Joy and pain. It's all part of life. It's all part of grandparenting. The good news is that the joy usually outweighs the pain.

*Part* 4

# *The Challenges of Grandmothering*

# Chapter 15

### ✒

# The Challenge of Discipline

THE BODY OF A MISSING FIVE-YEAR-OLD HAS BEEN FOUND. THE GRANDMOTHER HAS BEEN CHARGED WITH MURDER." Until these gruesome words came across the airwaves, Jan's thoughts had been on the hectic events of the day. She was in her car, rushing as usual to yet another appointment.

"It seemed my life had reached a stage that involved one mad dash after another," she recalled. "I felt so out of control, as if I were being swept from one event to the next on some big, relentless wave, seldom stopping long enough to look at what I was rushing toward. As she drove that day, she wondered, *Where have the years gone? My oldest son is thirty-three years old, one of my granddaughters is entering third grade, and I'm going to be fifty-six in a few months. How can it be?"*

The words from the news broadcast struck like a piercing arrow into Jan's heart, jarring her thoughts back to the present. What could have happened between that grandmother and her precious grandchild?

The report went on to say the little girl, who had been reported missing from a shopping mall the previous week, had been found along the roadside many miles from her home. Apparently the grandmother and aunt had faked a kidnapping story to cover up the death of the little girl. In fact, the grandmother had gone so far as to appear on newscasts pleading with the public for any word about her granddaughter.

Jan listened, bewildered by what she was hearing. *How could this be?* she wondered. *We believe the bond between a grandma and her grandchildren is so special that violence of any kind would be unthinkable.*

She suddenly remembered the grandma who recently had sat near her at a small restaurant. She certainly appeared frazzled. Jan had been watching her two-year-old granddaughter, Colleen, while Colleen's mother was getting her hair permed. Apparently this grandma was babysitting too. She cast knowing glances Jan's way, then glowered at the little one sitting at the table with her. He looked to be about two also, and was he fidgety! This small lunch place had no high chair or booster seats, so both Colleen and this other little one were sitting on regular chairs, with nothing to keep them in their seats.

Jan gave a knowing smile back at the other grandma, thinking they did have a lot in common. *We are both here because we want to be,* Jan had thought. Soon the other grandma warmed up to her and started making comments across the tables. "I can't believe I'm doing this again," she stated. "Look at him, candy all over his face, his feet dirty. He is the most active child I've ever seen."

Yes, she was right; he did have candy all over his face, his little bare feet were filthy, his clothes were rumpled, and was he ever active! Jan wondered who had given him the candy and who had let him run around with unprotected feet. Who was in charge of this little guy? She responded with an "uh-huh," and went on with her lunch. Colleen was really getting into her chicken-noodle soup by this time, dripping it here and there—they had no bib, and napkins were in short supply in the tiny eatery. Jan kept her attention focused on Colleen. She really didn't feel like talking and certainly didn't want to hear the negatives the other grandma was offering about her little charge.

But the other grandma did not let up. "Can you believe my daughter expects me to take care of him?" By now her little grandson was off the chair and onto the floor, taking his cookie with him. "You sit there!" she admonished him as she jerked him roughly back up onto the chair. "And if you get out of it again I will never take you anywhere with me ever again! Grandma is so sick and tired of your behavior. Now you just sit there!" Jan watched in horror, then looked at the lines drawn on the face of this grandmother. *Could I ever act like that to my grandchildren?* she wondered.

The scene got much worse, and the other grandma looked over at Jan as if to say, "Help me! I'm in trouble here, in trouble with myself, my daughter, and my grandson. What am I to do?" She finally gave up on the lunch, which had consisted of only a cookie for the little one, anyway; she gathered up her things and got up to leave. Then she took one whiff of her little grandson, and said, "Oh, no, that's the last straw!" She turned to me and said, "Can you believe it? He has dirty pants and I didn't bring any diapers with me! It's going to be two hours before we get home." Then she turned to the little one again. "You're a case. You really know how to get to me, don't you!"

Jan was embarrassed for the other grandma. She quietly tried to say that her daughter-in-law should arrive at any time with the car and that in Colleen's diaper bag would be extra diapers she would gladly share with the other grandma. But the woman only nodded and began to put the little one down, holding him at a distance. She grabbed his overall straps and dragged him roughly across the floor. "These straps really come in handy," she said as she bustled out the door.

Jan's face was burning as she turned her attention to little Colleen and looked into those precious deep-brown eyes; she wondered what Colleen thought about all that had gone on. Jan's thoughts focused on the rough treatment, violent words, and blaming that made up the world for the little boy with the dirty feet and the big blue eyes. Could he possibly have any chance at all of not repeating that world with his own children and then his grandchildren?

That disheartening scene was vividly replayed in Jan's memory as the words of the radio reporter rang in her ears. *A grandma murdered her very own grandchild.* Jan's mind flashed back to the grandmothers meeting we told you about in Chapter 2, a gathering of beautiful, precious grandmas, all wanting to be the very best grandmas they could possibly be. Could the grandma Jan met in the restaurant or even the grandma she heard about in the news have been in our group? She had to admit the possibility that these two grandmas had, at one time, really wanted to do their very best with their role of grandmother. There could have been a time when they wanted to care for their grandchildren as nurturers and love them into adulthood. What went wrong?

## Disciplining Ourselves

We are all capable of doing things we never thought we would do. How many women find themselves so rushed and stretched that their patience and gentleness are greatly sacrificed? We know that certainly happens to *us* from time to time.

When we grandmothers allow ourselves to become so overwhelmed by responsibilities and commitments that we find ourselves doing things and saying things we know we'll soon regret, we need to practice some swift *self*-discipline. That's when we must take a step back, think about what we're doing, and ask God to set a guard on our mouths. As grandmothers we should try our best to practice gentleness.

Remember that God will change the deepest part of you if you ask Him. But you must be prepared for the change; be ready. Don't ask for His help if you really don't want Him to change you.

## *Our Grandparenting Styles Affect Our Views on Discipline*

Most parents have strong feelings and opinions on the subject of discipline. But we grandmothers often see the matter very differently. We must be very careful as we walk the thin line between doing what we believe is best for our grandchildren and not alienating their parents. Let's first look at how the different styles of grand-mothering affect this matter of discipline:

A doer grandma is likely to be spur-of-the-moment in her approach to discipline. A lot depends on what mood she happens to be in. She tends to let the children go until things get serious, then she'll jump in with a sharp, "No! Stop that right now! Don't do it again!" It's important for doers to strive toward being more consistent in their expectations. It's only fair to let the kids know the rules ahead of time.

A dreamer grandmother is the one most likely to look at

whose feelings are going to get hurt, then base her discipline on that. If she thinks she is going to alienate the parents too much, she probably won't say anything. But if the child is really hurting, she will want to step in. Dreamers are the champions of the one in the most pain. Their struggle will be with their tendency to be too cautious to get involved.

A discoverer grandma tends to dwell on the principle of the thing. Almost anything a child does is all right as long as it doesn't violate a principle (honesty, for instance, or fair play). Even when the child might not understand the principle he or she is violating, a discoverer grandma might lash out with a scolding. Or she might withdraw from the child and tell somebody else to take care of him or her. It's important that discoverers help their grandchildren understand their expectations and the reasons for them.

A director grandmother is likely to lay down rules and laws according to the way she raised her own children or the way she thinks children should be raised today. *Should* is a key word for directors. The challenge for directors is to consciously work at developing flexibility within themselves and in their discipline of their grandchildren. But the strength here is that grandchildren of directors have the advantage of knowing where their boundaries lie.

## An Attitude of Discipline

Discipline is an important method of education. We want children to learn to behave properly, not just to stop misbehaving. We want them to learn that their actions will have consequences. We discipline them with the understanding that the sooner they learn these lessons, the happier their lives will be.

"The first time we kept our grandson Timmy overnight, he was only a year and a half," Betty recalls. "He fought and screamed at nap and bedtime. He refused to sit in his high chair during meals, and he drank his juice while running around on my pale blue carpet. My husband and I wondered how we were ever going to survive seven days.

"Actually, it turned out to be a wonderful week. Timmy ate all his meals at the table with us instead of in his high chair. He tried crying for a few minutes when he was put down for his naps or at bedtime, but when we didn't rush in and pick him up, he quickly fell asleep. Soon we had no fussing at naptime."

What happened? How did Betty change Timmy from an out-of-control child into a pleasant, happy little boy in one week's time? "It wasn't so much what we did or said to Timmy," Betty said. "It was what we had learned about discipline."

David Elkind, author and professor of child study at Tufts University, said in his book, *Grandparenting,* "The essence of sound discipline is not a set of techniques but rather an attitude that conveys to the child that we are in charge and that we know what we are doing."

Timmy realized that misbehaving with Grandma wasn't going to work. It wasn't that she had to scold him or punish him. She simply let her actions show that, although Grandma loved him very much, she meant business.

"As a parent, I didn't have that kind of confidence in my parenting ability," Betty admits. "I was too wrapped up in trying to find the right things to do. I felt insecure, and it came through loud and clear to my children."

Kids are much smarter than we realize. They know just how far to push us. With our experience, we understand several things that enable us to discipline differently: First, our self-esteem isn't all wrapped up in the child. Second, we know that children are very resilient. We may make mistakes, but with an abundance of love, those mistakes won't be fatal. Third, we know how important rules are, but we also know that rules can sometimes be bent, stretched, or broken.

## It's Different at Grandma's House

We know one long-distance grandmother who was going to have her three-year-old grandson and her one-year-old granddaughter come for a week while the parents were many states away. This grandmother hadn't ever had grandchildren stay overnight by themselves at her home. (She used to have the grandson stay overnight or for a weekend when he was younger and lived closer to them, but since his family moved so far away she hasn't done that.)

This grandma was panicked over the thought of the children being there for a week. What important discipline guidelines did she need to remember?

For example, there's the problem of putting the children to bed. Little J. T. doesn't want to go to bed. He will say, "Read me another story," but there's a point at which you can't read any more stories. At the parents' house, the mom and dad don't want Grandma to lie in bed with J. T. until he goes to sleep because it starts a pattern they have to follow. The mom (Grandma's daughter) did that and it was a problem. Yet it *is* a way to get over his screaming at bedtime, and Grandma knows she can handle it that way. *Maybe they don't like it at their house,* this grandma believes, *but when he's at my house it's different.* Her theory is, "At my house we do whatever works."

Betty sympathizes with this grandmother. "When Elizabeth's parents were in Europe for two weeks, she was very frightened. It was a long time for a little child under two to be away from her parents and she needed extra security. So we let her go to sleep in our bed, something we had not done with our children and we wouldn't normally do; but Elizabeth needed that security. If you try to just be tough with them when they are missing their mommy and daddy, and they're in a strange situation and not used to you, then you're setting yourself up for having more problems. Instead, surround them with love and tenderness, letting them know this is a special arrangement with certain boundaries in it."

Our little grandbabies have to be protected from the harsh realities of life. They may face toughness everywhere else, but Grandma's house is different. They need to feel safe at Grandma's house, especially when it's the first time they're staying overnight or for an extended time. When they're unsure, they need more reassurance and tenderness than usual.

Jan readily acknowledges the fact that her granddaughters get to do a lot of things at her house that they don't get to do at home. "But," she said, "we have an understanding about it." She tells Michelle, "You can do that here, but you might not be able to do it other places."

Michelle always giggles and says, "Oh, Grandma, I know that! That's why I like to come here so much." That's not to say Jan lets the girls do things their mother or father would *really* object to. But she does make special allowances that sometimes require extra time—or patience—and lets their time together be special.

"One of Michelle's favorite things is to play on the bed, jumping around with Molly, our little cocker spaniel. Now, I realize that most moms cannot allow jumping on the bed, and we do have our limits: no jumping in ways that might hurt Michelle or damage the bed." There are still rules; they're just a little less rigid.

Some grandparents see the issue differently. They believe the parents of their grandchildren do not set enough limits on their children's behavior. So to Grandma falls the distasteful job of trying to balance things out by being more strict than the children's own parents. Either way, it's difficult to balance grandmother rules against parent rules.

## Constructive Spoiling

You spoil your grandchildren? Great! That's a grandmother's special privilege. We consider grandchild-spoiling as an analogy to the grace of God, of getting something better than one deserves. We like to think of it as *constructive spoiling,* special attention that helps a child understand God's generous love. The Bible tells us that as sinners we deserve death. But God loved us so much He sent His only Son, Jesus Christ, to die so that we might have life. Maybe, in spoiling our grandchildren a bit, we can help them understand an important part of God's nature.

Constructive spoiling isn't about the material things we give our grandchildren. Instead, it's knowing what is important at a specific time and taking the time to look beneath the surface, seeking to understand the motivation for misbehavior.

### It Sets Limits

Constructive spoiling *does* set limits. Children want and need to know the boundaries. The memo on page 188 from a child to parents is from *Weathering the Storm: The Survival Guide for Teenagers* by Dan Clark (published by British American Publishing and distributed by Simon and Schuster); this excerpt was published in *Bottom Line Personal* newsletter. We believe it could be equally instructive to grandparents.

## Parental Authority

Constructive spoiling does not mean there are no rules. Certainly we need to be free to set rules for times when the children are with us. It's important to first ask the parents what rules they have, and then determine how adamant they are about your adhering to those rules. If you disagree with the parents, don't discuss it in front of the children. Tell the parents privately what you would like to do differently while the children are with you, then ask their permission to do it.

For instance, suppose your grandchildren's parents absolutely refuse to let their children have any junk food at all. But you are taking the children to the circus and you really want to buy them cotton candy. Talk it over with the parents. If they won't agree, respect their wishes, but ask them for some suggestions of a special treat. Perhaps a box of raisins or a package of unsalted peanuts would be a compromise. Or maybe parents will agree that a sweet treat is fine for a once-in-a-while occasion.

It is important that we resist the temptation to undermine the authority of our children's parents. One grandmother told about a Thanksgiving dinner when all the relatives had gathered around the table. Nine-month-old Becky, sitting on her grandmother's lap, wanted some of Grandma's dessert so Grandma gave her a bite of whipped cream. Baby Becky loved it and begged for more.

## A What-matters-most Memo
## from Child . . . to Parents (or grandparents)

**Don't spoil me.** I know quite well that I ought not to have all that I ask for—I'm only testing you—and . . .

☐ **Don't be afraid to be firm with me and set curfews and rules.** I prefer it. It makes me feel secure.

☐ **Don't protect me from consequences.** Sometimes I need to learn the painful way.

☐ **Don't let me form bad habits.** I rely on you to detect them in the early stages and give me direction by example.

☐ **Don't make me feel smaller than I am.** It only makes me behave stupidly to prove that I am "big."

☐ **Don't correct me in front of people if you can help it.** Praise in public. Chastise in private.

☐ **Don't make me feel that my mistakes are sins.** It upsets my sense of values.

☐ **Don't put me off when I ask questions.** If you do, you will find that I'll stop asking you and seek information elsewhere.

☐ **Don't tell me my fears are silly.** They are real to me and you can do much to reassure me if you try to understand.

☐ **Don't suggest to me that you are perfect or infallible.** It hurts and disappoints me to learn you are neither.

☐ **Don't be inconsistent.** That confuses me and makes me lose faith in you.

☐ **Don't ever think that it is beneath your dignity to apologize to me.** An honest apology makes me feel surprisingly warm toward you.

☐ **Don't forget that I can't thrive without lots of love and understanding.** I need your quantity and quality time and your affection.

☐ **Please keep yourself fit and healthy. I need you and I love you.** Please don't die early because you smoke, drink too much or use drugs.

☐ **Because "stuff happens," let's stick together.** I believe in you. I need you and hope you believe in me.

From *Weathering the Storm: The Survival Guide for Teenagers* by Dan Clark. Published by British American Publishing, 19 British American Blvd., Latham, New York 12110. $7.95. 518-786-6000. Distributed by Simon and Schuster.

Grandma had given her several more bites when her son-in-law abruptly got up from the table and stalked off into the bedroom. His wife followed after him.

For a moment Grandma couldn't figure out what was wrong. Then she realized she had unthinkingly fed Becky without asking permission. When her daughter returned, Grandma apologized. "Don't worry about it," her wise daughter said. "I explained to him that you love Becky as much as we do and that you would never give her anything you thought wouldn't be good for her. A little whipped cream isn't going to hurt Becky."

It's better to ask than to risk alienating parents.

When you are in your children's homes, be aware of their rules and be cautious about your actions and reactions. When your grandchildren sense they have you on their side in a family battle, you may be the one who ends up wounded in the cross fire. Statements such as, "Sorry, but your mother won't let me do that," or "Sure you can, but don't tell your daddy" makes their parents seem like the bad guys.

You say the parents are too strict? That they have too many unnecessary rules? Maybe so, but it is still better to follow their lead until you have a chance to discuss the issue with them privately. Some parents are willing to let Grandma relax the rules when she is visiting in their home. Others say it's okay for her to have different rules when the children are in Grandma's home. But whatever their decision, if you want to be a successful grandmother, your first rule will be to cooperate with the parents as best as you can.

What if your grandchildren are being raised in a home where there are no rules? What if they are allowed to do whatever they want to whenever they please? This can make visiting them, or having them as guests in your home, a miserable experience. But what can you do? When you are a guest in their home, you are not free to put demands and expectations on your grandchildren's behavior. You do, however, have the right to your privacy and to protect yourself and your property. For instance, it is up to you to decide whether or not the children are free to prowl through your handbag, suitcase, or personal cosmetics.

Often children who are raised in a home without boundaries long for guidelines. Although they may test whatever rules you lay down, if you lovingly and firmly state your boundaries and if you are consistent in sticking to them you will find the children usually will respect them.

When children who are not used to boundaries are visiting in your home, it is important for them to know that you love them very much, but there are things that are unacceptable in your house. Clearly point out what is off-limits and explain why. Be sure to balance these "can'ts" with "cans"—what they are allowed to do and where they can play. Begin with the positives, then add the limits. When they know you care about them and have planned special things for them, those off-limits areas won't be so enticing.

Betty recalls a time when her granddaughter, Toria, then three, came to visit. As Toria walked through Grandma's living room, she cautioned, "Be careful, Grandma's house has lots of breakfuls!" It wasn't a complaint; it was simply a statement of fact. "We all laughed at her description of my knickknacks, which I have chosen not to remove when the grandchildren visit," Betty said. "I have a special place for the grandchildren's toys. They know where that place is and they head for it immediately."

It is entirely possible for children to have a wonderful

time at Grandma's without Grandma having to clear out the house before they arrive.

One of the great joys of grandparenting is the fact that disciplining and training the children is not our responsibility. That's their parents' job. We can participate in teaching them, but it's not our burden. Much of what does come from us will be accomplished through modeling. How we act, how we react, and how we view life will have a great impact on our grandchildren.

If you have ever closely observed young children, you are probably as amazed as we are at how sensitive they are to what is going on around them. Even very young babies react to unspoken tension in a room. Often one or another of our grandchildren have voiced concern over a conversation he or she has overheard between adults who had no idea the child was within earshot. The attitudes you project when your grandchildren are around are probably more important than any rules you set.

## Methods of Discipline

Like wise parents, wise grandparents will have a treasure chest of discipline ideas. Investigate different ideas about praising them, rewarding them, or promising to spend time with them for good behavior, and taking away privileges or using time-outs when there's negative behavior.

Time-outs are more familiar to parents than to grandparents. Few of us knew about this idea in our parenting days. Yet, according to Ron Taffel, a psychologist and author of *Parenting by Heart,* time-outs are the kindest way of disciplining. He says time-outs work because they are boring and kids hate boring environments. That's why sending a child to his or her bedroom for a time-out isn't a good idea—there is too much to do in there! Other experts suggest having time-outs at a place near you, perhaps at the dining table, so the child still feels a part of the family.

If you want to investigate more ideas about time-outs, you might read *Time-Out for Toddlers: Positive Solutions for Typical Problems in Children,* by James Varni and Donna Corwin. We've included a few of their suggestions here:

## Modeling Your Attitude

A pivotal attitude is expecting the best of your grandchildren. This doesn't mean putting pressure on them to achieve and be the best in any particular area. It's just demonstrating your firm belief in their basic good. A nagging grandmother takes the joy out of the relationship. Our grandchildren deserve to be viewed from their highest potential.

We should be quick to forgive and always ready to encourage a child to try again when he or she has failed or disappointed us. Use positive, image-building words rather than negative putdowns or images. Offer corrections or suggestions in a positive manner rather than using such phrases as "you always" or "you never."

## Reducing Expectations

Many times our greatest disappointments come from unrealistic expectations. This is especially true if our grandchildren live quite a distance away and we don't get to see them very often. We dream of how wonderful our times together will be. We make plans so big and build hopes so high that the reality can't possibly measure up.

One grandmother told of her experience with her two grandchildren, ages five and seven, who were coming for

## Teaching a Quiet Discipline

Time-out is a disciplinary technique best used on children ages two through ten, according to *Time-Out for Toddlers: Positive Solutions for Typical Problems in Children* by James W. Varni and Donna C. Corwin. Their suggestions:

**1.** Buy a kitchen timer or any timer that dings.

**2.** Designate a corner for the timeout chair, preferably in a boring hallway or room that you can easily monitor. Do not use the child's bedroom.

**3.** Be sure to practice timeout steps with your child before you begin to use it.

**4.** Explain that when the child does something wrong, he or she will have to sit in the chair until the timer sounds.

**5.** When your child misbehaves, say exactly what was done wrong (for example, "You didn't pick up your toys when I asked you to").

**6.** Tell your child to go to the time-out chair, and help if needed. For instance, grasp the wrist gently but firmly and lead the child there.

**7.** Set the timer for one minute for each year of your child's life (for example, three minutes for a three-year-old).

**8.** Your child has to be quiet for at least thirty seconds before the timer goes off, otherwise reset it.

**9.** After your child has had several days of being quiet at least thirty seconds during the time-out periods, gradually increase the quiet time by thirty-second intervals until the child has to be quiet the whole time. Reset the timer when the child acts out in the time-out chair.

**10.** If your child gets off the time-out chair before the timer goes off, give one swat on the rear end and lead him or her back to the chair without saying a word.

a two-week visit. Grandma had worked hard making a small tablecloth, napkins, and apron, and planning a tea party for her five-year-old granddaughter. She had gathered together a stack of books she planned to read to the children. They were all going to go to the zoo and the park. What a perfect visit this was going to be!

The visit was a disaster. The kids were bored with everything. They fought with each other and argued with Grandma. They didn't want to eat what Grandma cooked. At night they missed Mom and Dad and couldn't get to sleep. To top it all off, Grandma lived in a retirement area where there were no other young children, and the other residents didn't appreciate the children's noise in the pool or want them playing on the surrounding golf course. What's a grandma to do?

This grandmother reassessed her expectations. She realized the children were feeling lonely and unsure of themselves. She had rushed in with her agenda too quickly and hadn't taken the time to find out their likes and dislikes. So Grandma backed off her nonstop schedule and gave the children time to adjust. She watched them, listened to them, and began to see what she could do differently.

"I learned a lesson in all this," the grandmother told us. "The fewer expectations I have, the better the visit will be."

Children are children, and being with them isn't always going to be wonderful.

"Every time I'm going to be with my grandchildren, I remind myself to get rid of my great expectations," Betty said. "Instead, I make a conscious decision to enjoy them and to savor the moment. Certainly I go ahead and make plans for things we can do together, but I keep those plans flexible."

Indeed, flexibility is a major key to enjoying grand-mothering. Let your grandchildren participate in setting the schedule. As much as possible, get your work done ahead of time so you can make the kids your number-one priority.

## Chapter 16

# The Challenge of Long-Distance Grandmothering

*T*wenty-five years ago, a job transfer took Betty and her family from Oregon to Arizona. "We were the first ones in either Fred's or my family to leave Oregon," Betty said. "We were a close-knit family, and it was so hard to go." What made it worse was that Betty's children were the only grandchildren and great-grandchildren her parents and grandmother had, and her little girls were the joy of their great-grandma's life.

Betty's grandmother was determined not to let distance interfere with their relationship. She called as often as she could, and every week cards or surprise packages arrived in the mail. Vacations and holidays were planned around being able to get together. "But," Betty said, "my grandma never quite forgave us for taking her babies away."

Betty's mother communicated with her granddaughters, too, not only by telephone and letters, but also by audio tapes. Every few weeks, Betty's mother would go to the library and bring home an armload of children's books. Then, indulging her love of drama, she would proceed to read the books on tape, complete with sound effects and picture explanations. Afterward, she would talk to the children, asking each one questions about school, activities, and so forth. She would also tell them stories about how things were when she was a child growing up in rural America.

Sometimes, as Grandma and Grandpa traveled around the country by car, they would prepare an ongoing travelogue for the children. They would describe the scenery and the weather, tell how far they traveled that day and how long it took, tell where they ate and what they had to eat, and finally give a description of where they stayed.

What blessed granddaughters Betty's girls were! And since the youngest was only eighteen-months-old when they moved, it was this constant contact with her grandparents' and great-grandparents' voices that allowed her to feel she knew them. She was so comfortable with them, in fact, that when she was barely three she spent a month with them without her parents or sisters.

"Until recently, our children haven't lived near any of their grandparents since the day we left Oregon," Betty said. "Yet I don't think their relationships could be any closer if we had stayed there."

If you, like most grandmothers today, have at least one grandchild who lives a good distance from you, you know how hard it is to say good-bye after a visit. Will that little one really be able to survive without his or her grandma? Can your child actually make it as a mother or father without your help? "From the first moment I saw my first grandchild, my thoughts were constantly on schemes to take me two thousand miles east to see him again," Betty said.

### That Tiny Baby

Perhaps the most frustrating period of long-distance grandparenting is during the infant years when the child is changing so rapidly. You can't even communicate with the little one at that age. Sure, pictures help and telephone calls and letters to Mama may keep you somewhat current on what is happening with the baby, but nothing takes the place of being there to hold that little one in your arms and coo and talk and sing to him or her.

Shortly after their second grandchild was born, Betty and Fred bought themselves a video camcorder. Trouble was, the only thing they really wanted to record was the grandchildren, and they were across the country. So the next time the family visited, Betty and Fred sent the camcorder home with them. "Next to being there, being able to view the videotapes of our grandchildren, seeing them in action as they grow and change, watching them take their first steps and hearing their first words, has been worth far more than the price of the camcorder," Betty said.

### As They Grow

When your grandchildren are younger than three and are away from you, it's not easy to do too much directly with them. However, audio tapes of you singing or talking to them will keep your voice familiar. It is helpful to supply your grandchildren with an up-to-date photo of you; the parents could show it to them whenever you call or when they listen to your voice on tape. One mother keeps a photo of her children's grandparents by their bed, and each night as the children say their prayers, she points out Grandpa Louie and Grandma Jean as they pray for them.

Older children love to get mail—though most never do. You can remedy that by buying colorful postcards and lettering simple messages on them. Even before they can read, children are enthralled by the colorful pictures and the fact that something actually came in the mail for them. Send them gifts in the mail that they can use and share with you. For instance, coloring books that have easy-to-remove pages and simple pictures could be sent with a set of crayons. Ask your grandchildren to send you back some of the pictures they have colored. As they begin to learn to read and write, find simple workbooks for their level and ask them to fill them in and return them to you so you can see how much they are learning.

When they begin to read, they may read their books aloud and have Mother record them. Before the tape is mailed, they can add to it, telling you all about school and what they are doing. If they find it hard to think of anything to say, send them a list of questions you would like answered. Be patient. They may be so busy playing with their friends or watching television they won't get around to answering your questions for several weeks.

If you know they have special interests such as ballet or soccer, look for little-known facts on these subjects and send them to your grandchildren. Children love to tell other children something they don't know. Inquire about their teams' names, or what kind of dances they are learning, or ask about other pertinent facts pertaining to their particular interests. Depending on the child's age, you might buy books, look for magazine or newspaper articles or video cassettes that tell the story of someone with interests like theirs who has done something special. Be careful, though, that you are showing genuine interest. Otherwise it may come across as pressure to meet unrealistic expectations.

Remember also that with children, out of sight is often out of mind. Don't be offended when your grandkids don't respond quickly with thank yous or letters and tapes. Continue to write and call and be interested, even if they don't seem very interested in you. By so doing, you are keeping the door open and reinforcing their security by showing them unconditional love.

This is only a beginning. The possibilities are limited only by your imagination. Are you determined that, even though you are a long-distance grandparent, you will play an important part in your grandchild's life? Are you ready to become involved? Great! Here are some more suggestions for you.

## Visiting with Grandma

By the time a child is five, he or she is usually old enough for a short visit to Grandma's house alone. Most airlines will give special attention to an unaccompanied child and will make sure he or she is picked up by the proper person at the other end. For an older child and a shorter trip, taking the bus or a train may be an option.

If you live within a two- or three-day drive from your grandchildren, you may decide to meet their family halfway between your homes, spend a weekend together, then take the grandchildren home with you for awhile.

Generally it is best to have just one grandchild visit at a time. A child can be more relaxed if he or she doesn't have to share Grandma and Grandpa with anyone else. That's not always true, of course. Sometimes the children can entertain each other and keep each other from getting homesick. But it is something to consider.

It's also helpful to set aside a "special" place that is just for your grandchildren. Having their own place, whether it is a separate room or simply a corner of yours, lets them know you have been looking forward to and planning for their visit. A new stuffed animal to sleep with, or an old favorite that always "lives" at Grandma's, helps them feel comfortable and at home. Don't feel obligated to keep your grandchildren busy every moment of every day they are with you. Allow them some time to do nothing, and allow yourself some time to tend to your regular hobbies or duties. If you know children who are close to your grandchildren's ages, you might arrange a picnic or a trip to the park with them.

When Betty's grandchildren were visiting from Texas, Jan arranged to pick up her granddaughter after school and we took them all to the beach. Jan packed juice and snacks, sand buckets, and cups. Betty brought Easter cookies she and her grandchildren had made that morning. It took the children awhile to overcome their shyness and inhibitions, but before the afternoon was over they were having a wonderful time.

### When You Visit Them

When you visit your grandchildren in their home, things won't be the same as when the children come to see you. At home the children will be in familiar surroundings with their own toys, their friends, and their schedules. They may prefer to play with their friends or watch television or read a book than give you all of their attention. Don't take this as a personal rejection. You may be the center of attention when you first arrive or when you do special things with them, but most of the time they are likely to take for granted the fact that you are there.

## Understanding Feelings

Don't be surprised or hurt if your grandchildren feel homesick sometime during their stay. The most typical times for homesickness to arise are when a child is over-tired or has been scolded or punished. At these times, try to put yourself in the child's shoes and understand how that little one is feeling.

We have both experienced situations like this. Sometimes we have handled them well, and other times we have handled them poorly.

"I remember one time when the grandchildren had been with us for over a week," Betty said. "We were all tired and tempers were fraying. My grandson was asleep, but my four-year-old granddaughter would not take a nap, nor would she stay in the room and lie quietly on the bed. I told her firmly what I expected of her, laid her down on the bed, and shut the door. Immediately she started crying and screaming and kicking the wall. She wanted her mama, and believe me, so did I!

"Determined not to lose my temper, but definitely fo-cused on winning, I strode into the room, picked the child up and sat with her on the bed. She continued to scream and kick, and she even tried to bite me. The way she was carrying on, you'd think I was beating her! I didn't try to talk; I just held her. After about forty-five minutes, she fi-nally quit struggling. I gently released my hold and started to talk to her calmly. Quickly she scrambled out of my arms and onto the floor on the other side of the bed. As I sat and watched and listened, her whimpers dropped off and she fell asleep.

"Only later did I realize that while I had not lost my temper or verbally or physically abused her in any way, my unspoken attitude had communicated frustration, disgust, and despair. I was focused on my own 'rights': the right to have a little rest in the afternoon, the right to expect my grandchildren to obey me, the right to be appreciated for all I had done for my granddaughter. Never once had I stopped to think how lonely she might be, how tired of living Grandma's way instead of Mommy's and Daddy's way."

If you realize you have handled a situation badly, don't despair. Consider it a learning experience and determine to be more sensitive the next time. Betty had the opportunity to try another approach about a week later. Once again her granddaughter was overtired and didn't want to rest. This time, instead of insisting on her way, Betty tried to find out what her granddaughter was feeling.

"Are you missing Mommy and Daddy a lot?" she asked.

"Yes," Toria hiccuped between sobs.

"Are you scared to move from your house in Tulsa to someplace new?"

"Uh-huh."

"Why are you afraid to move?" Betty asked.

"'Cause I'll miss my friend, Whitney. I won't have any friends in Texas," Toria replied.

As the conversation went on, Toria calmed down and dropped off to sleep. The difference? This time Grandma was trying to understand what her granddaughter might be feeling instead of determining to show her who was in control.

Understanding a child's feelings seldom comes naturally. It requires that we do two things: Listen very carefully to what the child is saying, and put what we hear the child say into words and feed them back to her.

If what we say back shows we don't understand what the kids are feeling, they will be blunt enough to let us know. This is not the time for glib answers: "I know just how you feel," or "You think that's bad? Why, when I was your age . . ." Take the time to probe deeply enough to find out exactly what your grandchildren are feeling, and acknowledge their right to have those feelings. Telling children, "You shouldn't be homesick," doesn't change the fact that they are. What it does do is cause them to feel guilty about their homesickness and leave them more upset than ever.

## Traveling Together

You may be able to spend time with your grandchildren by taking trips with them. When Betty was a child, her grandmother took her to Victoria, British Columbia, and they had high tea at the Empress Hotel.

"She took the opportunity to teach me about etiquette," Betty said, "old-fashioned ideas like the importance of wearing gloves and hats, and the proper way to hold a teacup and sip my tea." Betty's grandmother allowed little Betty to share "grown-up" experiences such as eating in fancy tearooms and restaurants. "These experiences taught me how to act in public and gave me an appreciation for fine service and elegant surroundings."

Other times Betty's grandparents took her to the mountains and taught her to appreciate the beauty of nature, and to catch, clean, and cook fish over an open fire. "From the beginning of my life to the end of theirs, traveling with Grandma and Grandpa was very special," Betty said.

One grandmother promised her grandchildren that when they got to be twelve, they would each be able to go alone on a trip with her and Grandpa. Knowing they would all have their turn, the grandchildren were able to plan where they wanted to go and save money for spending.

Taking your grandchildren along on trips doesn't have to be expensive. Let the child help you make plans that fit within your budget. If the child's parents are willing and able to help out with expenses, let them. Their contribution can make it possible for you to have a wonderful time together without struggling under a financial burden.

Letters, telephone calls, packages, and tapes from you. Perhaps videos from them. Visits and trips together. These ideas are a good start. But what other things might you do to keep the lines of communication open between you and your grandchildren who live far away?

Here are some suggestions:

1. Ask the children to send you their school photos every year. You might even offer to pay for them.

2. Occasionally buy a small gift certificate from a national fast-food chain that has an outlet in their hometown and treat them to lunch through the mail.

3. Send the children old photos of their parents as children. Fill in the backs with such information as the date the picture was taken, the parent's age, where the picture was taken, and the names of others in the picture. Also send them old photos of you and Grandpa, and the places you lived as a child.

4. Send them snapshots of you or other family members who live in your area, along with pictures of interesting places you might take them when they visit.

5. If your area specializes in certain crops that can be shipped, try sending them a box of that specialty (fruit or nuts, for instance). If you make jams or jel-

lies, or if you can fruit or make special baked goods, occasionally surprise them with a homemade gift package just for them. (Priority Mail usually arrives within two days and isn't prohibitively expensive.)

6. If your grandchildren are into computers, you might be able to share a new computer program or game with them.

7. Sending interesting articles or funny cartoons from your hometown newspaper shows your grandchildren you are thinking of them even when you are reading the paper.

8. Find out what your grandchildren's favorite television programs are. Try watching them and then commenting on them to the children. Or you might ask them what they think about situations presented on the show.

9. Send each child a few stamped, self-addressed envelopes, and ask them all to send you photos, clippings, artwork, or whatever is interesting them currently.

10. Ask them about their favorite musicians and listen to their music. Share your favorite music with them and tell them why you like it. Ask them why they like their favorite.

11. If you are patient enough, sometimes it is fun to go through magazines and paste together letters, using pictures to replace some of the words. Or try writing a letter in a circle, round and round and round. Children really enjoy creative letters.

12. Send "secret pal" cards, letters, postcards, or gifts to your grandchildren. Kids love secrets, even if they figure out it's from you.

When we live a long distance from our grandchildren, it takes time and effort to develop and keep a strong relationship with them. But how else are we to be an influence in their lives? How else can we demonstrate the traits we would like them to adopt as their own? How else will they ever know how important they are to us and how much we love them?

One young grandmother told us she had a very lonely and unhappy childhood. But every summer she got to travel to her grandparents' house and spend two weeks with them. "They were so full of love and joy and gladness," she said. "For two weeks every summer, I learned that life really could be loving and good. My grandmother wasn't around most of the year, but she was the one who gave me the gift of hope."

Such is the power of long-distance grandmothering.

# Chapter 17

# The Challenge of Filling the Gap

*eing a grandparent is not all it's cracked up to be. When you hear the word* **grandmother,** *a picture comes to mind of a wrinkled, gray-haired, smiling lady wearing an apron and bustling around the kitchen baking cookies for her grandchildren or feeding birds in the park or buying out the toy store to make the little ones happy. The truth is, being a grandparent is far more difficult than being a parent.*

*As a grandmother, I am not only struggling with the problems of my age, I am also dealing with my daughter's problems and those of my grandchildren. I don't have the money to spoil the kids and I don't have the time or energy to be the sweet, cookie-baking grandma. I have no solutions for my daughter's marital or financial problems. I've had trouble finding the right discipline for my grandsons that will send them on to responsible adulthood. I lose my cool frequently and then feel guilty about it. Never was I this stressed when I was a single parent.*

*Don't misunderstand. I love my children and my grandchildren, and I am fortunate to be able to see them on a daily basis. But often it's only by the grace of God that I manage to get through the day.*

So went the letter we received from a woman who had written to us about some extremely tough times her family was struggling through. We appreciate her honesty. There probably isn't a grandmother alive who hasn't at some time felt at least a little of what this grandma was experiencing. But most of us are hesitant to admit that at times the joys of grandmothering can be overshadowed by the cares and burdens of life.

Betty clearly recalls the early-morning telephone call from a good friend who announced with sadness and confusion that she was going to be a grandmother—in two weeks. "I knew her children," Betty said, "and none of them was married. My heart ached for her as she told her story of bitter disappointment and broken dreams. To be hit with the news that her daughter was about to become a single mother was devastating, and to have been excluded from the news until the very last minute seemed like a personal betrayal."

The fact is, in our circles of friends, we know several women who have had to face similar circumstances. We can all understand the pain grandmothers feel when things don't go the way they "should." We start out certain that our families will beat the odds. They will stay together, happily living out their lives, joyfully celebrating special occasions together for years and years and years to come. Then suddenly, at some point, the realities of life confront us and the unthinkable happens. We watch helplessly as our children make the same mistakes we made—and sometimes act on decisions we would never have acted upon. Sometimes the results are so critical that the well-being, even the very lives, of our grandchildren are threatened. After telling us their stories, grandmothers cry out, "How can we live with this?"

## *The Painful Facts of Life*

Perhaps you will identify with some of the issues we will talk about in this chapter—divorce, death, and substance and physical abuse. The grandmothers who endure these tragedies are special women who love their children and grandchildren despite the painful situation. If these facts of life don't hit your family, families close to you are sure to be affected. Perhaps the following descriptions will give you insight into their problems and encourage you to be an encouraging and supporting friend.

## Divorce

"She was lying in the corner, curled up in a little ball, holding her knees to her chest and sobbing desperately. Her face was turned to the wall as though she wanted to shut out the world." An anguished grandmother was telling us about her three-year-old granddaughter whose world split in two when her mom and dad were divorcing.

"I thought my heart would split as well," this grandma recalled. "I felt so helpless. I had an overwhelming urge to just run away and take my granddaughter with me. Every time I tried to soothe or comfort her, she lashed out at me in anger." After a pause in her storytelling, the distraught grandmother added softly, "I was just like her. Inside of me there was a tight curled-up ball of anger and hurt, too, and it wanted to lash out and scream at everyone, even those who wanted to help me."

How terribly painful it is to be caught in the cross fire of a son or daughter and their mate who are tearing each other apart, so absorbed in their own pain and grieving they give little thought to the wreckage they leave in their paths. We are horrified at the deep hurt our grandchildren suffer. And we feel used and taken aback that someone who was brought into our family to love and care for is now being torn away.

"I didn't dare pressure my granddaughter to talk, so for close to an hour we lay there together," this grandmother told us. "Finally the little one rolled over and faced me, and I said, 'Hey, kid, let's go make some popcorn.' It sounds strange, but it made more sense to distract her than to press her to talk when the time wasn't right."

Grandmother after grandmother told us that the dilemma of dealing with an ex–daughter-in-law or ex–son-in-law was one of the toughest things they were ever called upon to do. Some said they were so, so angry at their son or daughter or at their child's former spouse they could not talk easily about them. In contrast, some said they "held on" to their child's former mate, not just because of the grandchildren, but because they hadn't been able to simply shut off the love they had for that person. One grandmother told us, "When I look in my date book and see that my ex–daughter-in-law's birthday is coming up, I literally get sick inside. I want so much to let her know I love her, but I'm always torn apart knowing that I need to move on and let her move on. I end up buying her a card saying 'to my special friend.' But I know in my heart she is much more than that. She is part of my 'heart family.'"

There is no comfortable place for children who are experiencing the separation or divorce of their parents.

It's as if they were living on a bridge; they don't belong

on either side of the stream. And because they don't belong on either side, they often end up building their own little house of protection somewhere on that bridge, somewhere secret from those who are on either side. Even Grandma might not be allowed into that house, especially if she gets involved in the fight. On the other hand, if Grandma is safe enough to trust, she may be the only one allowed in.

It's hard to stay out of the fight. You see things, and you understand things. But remember, more than anything else, children caught in a fighting family need a safe place. They need adults who can be there in the bridge house with them.

"When one of my children went through a divorce, I thought I would literally die from the pain," Jan said. "I didn't think either my granddaughter or her parents would survive it either. I was convinced there would never be a time when any of us would feel decent or have a sense of family again."

Jan had to learn from other grandmothers who had gone through the divorce of their kids. Here are some of the principles she found especially helpful in getting through this incredibly painful period:

1. Don't take sides, even though one of the divorcing parents is your child. Sometimes it's easier to get angry at our sons or daughters rather than at their mates. Try to stay objective.

2. Affirm your grandchildren's loyalty to both parents. Talk to them about the positive things you see in their relationship with both Mom and Dad.

3. Let your grandchildren know you are in the middle, just as they are. Let them know you understand how

it feels to love two people who are fighting each other.

4. Work through your own pain by talking to someone outside the family. Find other grandmas who are going through the same thing and can understand your frustrations.

5. Model forgiveness as a principle for all involved. Know that forgiveness takes time and that the hurts are not easily forgotten. Above all, don't hold grudges.

6. Ask God to heal you, your children, and your grandchildren of the injuries caused by divorce.

We do not always have the ear of our children or our children's mates, but we often do have the ear of our grandchildren. We can let them know we understand they are hurting. We can tell them we are hurting too. Staying involved with them and talking about the situation may be one of the most healing steps God uses to put our lives and theirs back together.

You say you've tried but your grandchildren just shut you out too? That really hurts. But if that happens, please understand this has much more to do with the depth of their hurt and frustration than it has to do with you. They still need you desperately. Don't quit letting them know how much you love them.

## With Divorce and Remarriage Come Step-Grandchildren

It may be that your child has remarried and you now are a step-grandmother. It may be that your family is in a wonderful situation. For many it does not. It may be that you have been called upon to accept changes you don't like at all. Your major challenge then is to love, accept, and create a safe place for the new people who have come into your life. It's not always easy, we know. But many grandmothers, when they open their hearts to those God places in their paths, find that God provides them with enough love to share, often far exceeding anything they ever thought possible. Remember to model a forgiving lifestyle.

## Death

"Jessica and Jamie now live on the West Coast," one grandmother told us sadly. "I miss them so! I hurt for me, but I also hurt for them. Not only did they lose their mother, now they have lost their grandparents too! And I have not only lost my daughter, I have lost her children."

This dear woman's daughter developed cancer when she was barely thirty years old. After two years of incredible suffering, she died. During those two years, Jessica and Jamie became very attached to their grandparents. They were with them nearly every day, and they shared the pain of watching their mother die.

"We talked together, we cried together, and we grieved together," this grandmother told us. "Their dad poured himself into his work—it was his way of coping with his own grief, I'm sure. But one month after my daughter died, he decided to take the kids and move to the other side of the country!"

Both grandparents and grandchildren were shocked and heartbroken, but nothing they could say made any difference. Dad had made up his mind this was the best way for him to start a new life for himself and the kids. "We knew it was the very worst thing he could do for the children, but his counselor told him he should 'do what he had to do.' We were outraged! The kids were in a good school situation here and were surrounded by supportive friends and understanding teachers. And they had loving grandparents who wanted more than anything to be there for them. But their dad took them away. My confidence in God's plan had already been shaken so badly, and now this. How could a loving God allow it?"

Another woman told us this story: "My son was killed by a drunk driver two years ago, and he left a beautiful wife and three great kids. I have been so paralyzed ever since his death that I don't think I can ever really live again. People tell me that I have to get on with my life, but how can I? My daughter-in-law is in a new relationship and I know the kids are really angry about it. They don't like her boyfriend at all. I watch them being dragged along in this, and I just can't bear to see them hurt again. If only she would wait a little while longer, until the children are better adjusted and a little older. They are so young, so vulnerable. I grieve over them every day. I know I'm not much help, but I just can't get a handle on my life anymore, physically or spiritually."

These two grandmothers have been called upon to live through what has to be the most hurtful thing a human being can endure—the death of a child. Regardless of the child's age, grieving parents all agree it brings forth pain like nothing else can. To lose a child is so against everything we believe about life. Children are supposed to outlive their parents, and certainly their grandparents. When they don't, it seems so totally unjust and unacceptable. We struggle to survive emotionally, knowing there is no way to ever make sense out of what has happened.

Grandmothers who talked about losing a grandchild expressed the same sort of painful grieving process. They grieved for themselves and they grieved for the hurting parents. One grandmother told us, "I'll never forget the horrible day my son called and said, 'Mom, I'm here at the hospital. Amy was hit by a car, and they don't think she's going to make it. Please pray.'

"I thought my insides were going to cave in. *It can't be,* I told myself. *Amy is so sweet, so perfect, her tiny three-year-old body can't be injured. Why, God, why?*

"I rushed to telephone my husband, and he said to meet him at the hospital. My thoughts just tumbled over and over. *What were we going to do? Would the doctor be competent? How would we ever tell the other children? Surely, there has to be hope, yet Danny's words sounded so final.*

"I got to the hospital too late. Amy had died on the operating table. Every bit of energy I had left went into comforting my son and his wife. The days that followed were a blur. It wasn't until months later that I allowed myself to really grieve. I am still hurting and still grieving, but my anger has finally subsided. I'm just now beginning to let God into my grief."

Anger. It is such a natural emotion, yet such a killer. Jessica and Jamie's grandmother told us, "I asked God time after time, and He is helping me begin to let go of my anger. Finally I am able to ask Him for a perspective that will allow me to build back the faith I once had in Him. It took a long, long time, and I'm sure it was the most difficult thing I'll ever do. Yet I'm convinced God uses time to heal even our deepest hurts. Over time I have been able to build back my own life and to take the energy I once gave to hanging on to my bitterness and use it to pray for those precious grandchildren who are so far away. I talk to them often and make sure they know there are two people here who love them intensely, and that we will be right here if they ever need us."

## Abuse

Two little identical boys sat very still and awaited their turn on stage. Each of the twins was dressed in short black pants and black-and-white-checked jackets; red bow ties set off their scrubbed cherub-like faces. As parents and grandparents pressed into the crowded auditorium, all straining their necks to see the kindergartners perform their parts in the school Christmas program, J. J. and J. P. sat together, shy and quiet, in the center of the first row.

No one in that audience would have guessed what the nicely dressed couple in their early sixties, sitting in the back row, were living through. They fit right in with all the other proud grandparents sprinkled throughout the audience. Like the other grandparents, they were bursting with pride. But inside, they were aching. Their son was in jail and their daughter-in-law was hiding somewhere, strung out on drugs. Grandma and Grandpa were battling for custody of the precious twins.

Over their short lives, these little ones had periodically been yanked out of their grandparents' home and thrust into the terrifying world of cocaine: living out of their father's car, watching Daddy beg for money, being beaten by a mother too intoxicated to realize she was hitting them for acting like normal little boys.

Grandma and Grandpa struggled to understand what had gone wrong.

In a December 16, 1991, *Newsweek* article entitled "Silent Saviors," Linda L. Creighton wrote that 3.2 million children in the United States live with their grandparents, an increase of almost 40 percent in the last decade. Four percent of all white children and 12 percent of all black children live with their grandparents. Millions more live with their grandparents part-time.

One grandmother told us, "The hardest thing I have ever had to do was to go to court and fight my own daughter for the custody of her two little boys. My daughter has had several problems with the law and is now out of prison on bail. She has no concept of mothering her children. She is irresponsible and abusive, and she refuses to go for counseling even though we have offered to pay for it.

"The boys are known as such behavior problems, no teacher wants them in class. My husband and I want very much to salvage these precious children if we can. We love them so much, but I'm really scared because I don't know if I can handle it. After just a few weeks, I can already feel myself breaking down. Where can I go to get help for them and for ourselves? The court costs were so outrageous we have no money left to raise the boys. I know God will give us the strength and courage to do the job, but honestly, I'm just so tired!"

How we wish we had a good, pat answer for this aching grandma. But the unfortunate fact is that grandparents who parent grandchildren just don't get much help from our social service system. Many grandmothers and grandfathers are extremely frustrated and feel helpless as they battle a system that does not always recognize their importance in a child's life.

Not only do parenting grandparents need support from governmental agencies, they need it from their families and friends as well. One grandmother who is raising three little ones told us her friends don't understand at all.

"They say if I'm so tired, I should just put them some-where else. But how can I? I love them!"

Yet there are some glimmers of light. In many areas, sup-port organizations are being formed. We will include some of them later in this chapter.

## *What Are My Rights as a Grandmother?*

In your efforts to be a grandmother who makes a posi-tive difference, some of you are in the frustrating and tragic position of wrestling with the legal system.

"Children should have the right to have shared memo-ries and experiences with their grandparents . . . and the opportunity to experience that kind of unconditional love," says attorney Richard S. Victor, founder and execu-tive director of the Grandparents' Rights Organization (GRO) and former president of the Family Law Section of the Michigan State Bar. Victor, quoted in Nancy Day's arti-cle "I Want to See My Grandchildren" in the November 25, 1991, issue of *Family Circle* magazine, said, "If this experience is being denied because of the death of a grand-parent, that's a tragedy. If it's because of family bickering or vindictiveness, that's an injustice."

Because of grandparents like the ones we've heard from in this chapter, the laws are changing. Today, several state supreme courts have supported grandparents' visitation rights when it's in the best interest of a child and every state now has a law that allows grandparents to petition for visitation rights. But because there are no standards, the laws vary widely from state to state. Currently, when grandparents live in a different state from their children, the rights granted in one state may not be enforceable in another. In half the states, the law allows visitation only if the children's parents have divorced or if one or both of them have died. If the family is intact, and the parents choose not to allow the grandparents to contact their grandchildren, the courts generally will not intervene.

The U.S. Supreme Court has declined to rule on this issue so, for now at least, grandparents' visitation rights remain in the hands of the states.

Even if grandparents are successful in legally gaining the right to see their grandchildren, the related court battles are long, disruptive, and very costly. If you are being denied the right to see your grandchildren, seek wise legal counsel. Contact your local bar association for a referral to a family-law attorney who has experience in third-party parental visitation rights.

When you meet with your attorney be sure you have documented evidence and a list of witnesses who are prepared to support your claim that it is in the best interests of your grandchildren to see you. The legal standard in most states seeks evidence that you had a consistent, caring relationship with them in the past. It will be up to you to prove this.

Your attorney may advise you to seek mediation before going to court. Or it might be that a minister, priest, social worker, or family therapist could help. Use the courts only as a last resort.

## In Separation or Divorce

If your grandchildren's parents are breaking up, ask them for a provision in the separation or divorce agreement that will allow visitation rights for both sets of grandparents.

If the parent who has custody remarries, give the new marriage time to work. Don't be too quick to jump in and aggressively press your visitation rights. Never undermine one of the children's parents, no matter how strongly you may feel about what he or she is doing. These times are tough enough for children who are probably feeling torn by loyalty to the divorced or deceased parent without your making it harder for them. Make an effort to keep the lines of communication open. If you and the children's parents simply cannot talk, call in a third party. Often the parents are simply afraid you are going to talk against them to the children. Seek to have an open discussion with the parent who has custody. Be willing to let that parent lay the ground rules, then follow them.

If there is animosity between you and the children's parents, take every precaution to ensure this does not involve the children. It is never in their best interest to try to transfer their loyalty from their parents to you. Visitation rights do not supersede parental rights, except when there is a threat to the children's safety.

## When There Is Neglect or Abuse

With the elaborate system of child protection and support agencies we have throughout our land, it doesn't seem there should be any difficulty intervening in a situation of child neglect or abuse. After all, weren't these agencies set up to protect and rescue the children?

Unfortunately, many seem to be more of a hindrance than a help. One woman told us she has been fighting the system for five years trying to gain custody of her nine-year-old granddaughter. Both the child's parents are addicted to crack cocaine and their mother is in prison. The father wanted the children, and the court agency ruled they had to go live with him. Six months ago, the six-year-old son was beaten to death by his father and the young girl was placed in a home for abused children where she tested positive for gonorrhea. She had been raped by one of her father's friends. As of this writing, the distraught grandmother is still seeking to gain custody of her grand-daughter.

For those grandparents who do get custody of their grandchildren, the financial support they get—if any—is less than one-third the amount available to foster families: The national average is $109 monthly for grandparents who are the sole care givers, compared with $371 monthly per child for foster parents. Many of these care-giving grandparents are retired and living on fixed in-comes. They never expected the financial responsibility of raising another family. About half of these families include both grandparents, but most of the other half are sup-ported by a grandmother alone.

Because of the unique pressures of raising grandchil-dren, several organizations have arisen around the coun-try. If you would like to be part of such a group, or if you would be willing to help start one, here are some organiza-tions that can help:

### GAP (Grandparents as Parents)
Psychiatric Clinic for Youth
2801 Atlantic Avenue
Long Beach, California 90801
310–933–3151

### Grandparents Raising Grandchildren
Attention: Barbara Kirkland
P. O. Box 104
Colleyville, Texas 76034
817–577–0435

**Second Time Around Parents**
Attention: Michele Daly
Family and Community Services of Delaware
    County
100 W. Front Street
Media, Pennsylvania 19063
215–566–7540

## "Throwaway" Children

A grandmother named Carolyn wrote to us about a child her son, then a teenager, had fathered out of wedlock. The child's mother had kept him until he was six, but from then on little Dale was bounced from foster home to foster home. As an adolescent, he became a chronic runaway. One day, without warning, he showed up on his grandmother's doorstep. Because he was a runaway, she contacted the local agency for help. They gave her none.

Carolyn soon became aware of the terrible discrepancies in laws that govern children dubbed "throwaways" by law-enforcement authorities. Because they have run away voluntarily, police will not search for them. If and when they are found, they are simply returned to the home or center from which they ran away, a situation that often has been abusive.

Dismayed, Carolyn decided to do some investigating and try to find a residential treatment center that could take care of Dale and give him the counseling he needed so badly. Finally she found one that had space and promised to help. She drove Dale to the facility, two and a half hours north of her home, kissed him good-bye, and left him. Two days later, he ran away again.

When Carolyn didn't hear from Dale, she grew frantic. Yet no one seemed to care, and no one would help her trace the boy. Finally, months later, Dale called. He was hungry, lonely, and wanted to come back to his grandmother's house. She sent him the bus fare.

That was a year ago. Here's a letter we just received from Carolyn:

*It occurred to me that since I shared so much of the bad news with you, it was only fair to tell you the good news. When I wrote to you last July I was at my wit's end. I didn't know what to do with this runaway grandson of mine. I decided that maybe for the time being the answer was to keep him here with me instead of trying to place him in residential treatment. He wasn't staying there anyway, and I was afraid something terrible would happen to him on the streets.*

*In a sense, I guess I finally gave up, or so it might appear to others. I decided I would expect nothing from him as long as he stuck around here. At least he would be alive, and with time, an answer to his problems would present itself. I prayed a lot, wearily telling God I had tried everything I knew how to do, now I didn't know what else to try and He would have to work it out. After all, Dale is His child too.*

*Well, a miracle happened. Dale began to settle down and relax when I told him I was going to keep him, but he would have to promise not to run away again. Though he wouldn't stay in school last year, this year he entered high school and I was able to get him into a special education program. When school started I braced myself for the worst, but much to my surprise, once he entered these classes, he was eager to go. When he had the flu and I had to keep him home, I practically had to hold him down because he wanted to go to school! I had an early Christmas present two weeks ago when he brought home a report card with three Bs, and two Cs! Quite a change from the six Fs he brought home last year.*

*His whole attitude seems to have changed. He was such a tough guy when I took him in last April. Now he's like most normal teenagers; he has friends, he's going to football games, and he's talking to girls on the phone almost every evening. Thank goodness for call-waiting. I would never get a call through otherwise! I don't care, it's a small price to pay for having him home with me at night instead of some of the places he's been in the past.*

*There is still lots of work to do. Dale's not completely out of the woods. He has years of anger stored up. I have him in therapy and the psychologist says it will take many years to work out the damage that has been done to him throughout his short lifetime. Being abandoned by both parents has done a lot to wreck his self-esteem, and his treatment in foster care made things even worse. At least we've made a start, and I know that with God's help Dale now has a chance to make it.*

*I still feel there is a lot to do toward changing the laws affecting children, particularly runaways. But I don't know how to do it. The way it stands now, we've really left our children up for grabs. Once out on the streets they are easy prey for the deviants who roam around looking for opportunities such as these. Some of Dale's friends have run away in the past few months and a few have gotten into bad situations, especially the girls. These kids think they know what they're doing, but they don't. We should be protecting them from themselves until they have a chance to grow up. But, as it stands now, there isn't anything to stop them—it's not against the law to run away.*

*Two months ago Dale admitted he had been molested. It was just as I suspected. The man up north who had befriended him when he was on the streets and had bought him food and clean clothes had also repeatedly molested him. He also gave Dale lots of alcohol. I contacted the authorities and the man has been arrested and will go to trial next week. Dale doesn't look forward to testifying against him. It will be embarrassing, he says. But he knows it has to be done.*

Carolyn, like so many other grandparents, was willing to get involved in what seemed like a hopeless situation. Although it seemed her every move was thwarted and the agencies set up to help were more of a hindrance, she never gave up. It has not been easy. Carolyn has paid a high price mentally, emotionally, and financially. Yet, in her own words, she doesn't doubt that the effort has been well worth it.

Carolyn continues to search for ways to make a difference. Currently she is putting Dale's story in writing with the hope that she can perhaps make a few teenage boys or girls think twice about engaging in irresponsible sexual activity.

To become involved in your grandchildren's lives during difficult times is not an easy decision to make. Yet over and over we have heard testimonies from people whose lives might have been truly tragic if, somewhere along the way, a caring and concerned grandparent had not made this choice. If you are facing such a situation, here are agencies that might help you make a wise, informed decision:

### Grandparents' Rights Organization (GRO)

555 S. Woodward Avenue, Suite 600
Birmingham, Michigan 48009
313–646–7191
Send a stamped, self-addressed envelope to receive information about this organization.

### Scarsdale Family Counseling Service

405 Harwood Building
Scarsdale, New York 10583
Write to request a free copy of the semi-annual newsletter *Grandparents in Divided Families.* Subscriptions are $10 per year.

*Family Law Quarterly,* Spring 1991, Volume 25, Number 1
This legal journal costs $9.50 plus $2.00 for shipping. Write to:
Order Fulfillment
American Bar Association
750 N. Lake Shore Drive
Chicago, Illinois 60611
312–988–5555

We wish God's special blessings on each and every one of you special grandmothers as you work to make a positive difference in the lives of your grandchildren.

# Chapter 18

# The Challenge to Pray

*A*re you listening to me, Grandma, or are you praying?" little Michelle asked. She was trying to tell Grandma Jan something and Grandma, a bit distracted, didn't respond as she usually did. It was Wednesday, always a special day for Grandma and her then six-year-old granddaughter. On Wednesdays Michelle gets out of school at noon, so Jan picks her up and brings her to Jan's house, where they do something special for the afternoon.

"We sure can pack the time full!" Jan said. "Sometimes we make a quick list of the things we want to do right away so we don't waste time. Other times we just sit quietly together, play with the dog, have a snack, and before we know it it's time to go. On the way back to Michelle's house, we always sing and pray."

"We don't always pray out loud, however," Jan said. "Sometimes I just reach over and lay my hand on Michelle's head and she gets quiet and says, 'What are you praying now, Grandma?'" Jan said.

Our grandchildren need a lot of things from us, but more than anything else, they need us to pray for them. Both of us firmly believe prayer is the foundation of God's plan in creating grandmothers. Grandmothers who pray faithfully for their grandchildren give them the most precious gift that can be given—an invitation for God to do His work in the lives of those young ones.

## *Teach Me to Pray*

The idea for a book on grandparenting first came to us through our time of shared prayer. For more than ten years, we have met together once a week to share and to pray. As our children married and began to have children of their own, we found more and more of our prayer time was concentrated on our children and grandchildren.

Because prayer has played such a central part in both our lives, we were impressed with the lady at our grandmothers meeting who requested, "Please include a section in your book on how to pray." Then she told us, "I pray, but I hear other people talk about answers to their prayers, and I couldn't say I have any real answers. My prayers don't seem to make a difference. I would like to know more about prayer."

Other grandmothers agreed. They said they tried to pray, but had trouble staying with it. They said their grandchildren needed their prayers. They said they wanted to experience "life-changing" prayer, but they just didn't know how to go about it.

"I was so glad to hear their interest," said Jan, "for I see prayer as the whole basis of my relationship with my grandchildren."

We like the way O. Hallesby describes one aspect of prayer in his classic book *Prayer,* written around the turn of the century: "Prayer is simply letting Jesus into your needs."

## So It's All Up to Me?

Actually, no, although this is a common misconception. Certainly prayer requires effort and discipline on your part. But it is God who initiates it. He places a hunger deep within us to have communication with Him, then He waits for our response. And as we learn to respond to Him in prayer, we find ourselves gaining a new perspective on life. We begin to understand how God penetrates every minute of every day of our lives. No longer can He be confined to far-off churches and liturgies. No longer is He merely a concept to be believed or disbelieved. Now He is present in our lives, living in us and through us as we go about our daily business.

It's not all up to you. But it is up to you to respond.

## But God Doesn't Answer My Prayers

Preacher Charles Spurgeon once said, "Prayer is the slender nerve that moves the muscles of omnipotence."

Most of us believe that God is all-powerful and that He could change things in our lives and in the lives of our grandchildren if He wanted to. So why doesn't He? Why don't our prayers move His muscles to action?

Scriptures teach us an interesting thing: God is equally kind and good and just and merciful whether He grants us our prayers or not. When He does grant our requests, it's because He loves us. When He does not grant them, it's also because He loves us.

"What?" you say. "That doesn't make sense."

It *is* hard to understand. The thing is, we're seeking answers with our finite human minds. That puts us at a distinct disadvantage to God, who answers with omnipotent wisdom.

When drug addiction touched their family, Jan and her husband prayed faithfully for healing. Every time they tried to remember that God *was* working in their lives (even though they didn't see anything happening), that old feeling that God had forgotten them would swoop down and engulf them once again.

"Again and again we had the whole scenario set up so perfectly," Jan recalled. "We'd say, 'Now, God, this is a really good time to act. Can't You see it? Don't You understand we're really at the bottom this time? We can't go on another day.'"

But God had His own time schedule, one Jan and Dave couldn't comprehend. That's how it usually seems to be. When we are praying to God to change people or circumstances, He never seems to do it in our way or within our time frame.

Are you discouraged because God doesn't seem to be answering your prayers? It may help to simply pray that God will allow you to see that He is involved. Just to be able to catch little glimpses of how His hand is on this person or how He is involved in that situation can give you great comfort and assurance.

### Relinquishment

The key to all answered prayer is relinquishment, to give up completely, to leave behind. Yet we are often our own worst enemies. We want things done our way, and we want them done *now.* This is particularly true of the prayers that surround our children and grandchildren. If we do relinquish our dear ones to the Lord, we often find it's not long before we snatch them back. This temptation seems to confront us most when we think our children and grandchildren aren't listening to God. We understand that God will not overrule our free will, yet we have no problem trying to overrule the free will of our kids, so we step in and try to take God's place in their lives.

We have learned to overcome this tendency ("At least most of the time," Jan and Betty said) by practicing a way of life and prayer described in *Cycle of Victorious Living,* written many years ago by Earl Lee. The process is based on selected verses from the 37th Psalm:

> Delight yourself in the LORD
> > and he will give you the desires of your heart.
> Commit your way to the LORD;
> > trust in him and he will do this:
> He will make your righteousness shine like
> > the dawn,
> > the justice of your cause like the noonday
> > sun.
> Be still before the LORD and wait patiently for
> > him. . . . (vv. 4–7, NIV)

Here's how it works: "I take my problem, whatever it is, and I figuratively lay it out on my hands, palms facing upward. I specifically state what it is, then I turn my hands down, with my palms open, and let the problem drop into God's hand. I commit the problem to Him. Now I have relinquished my problem to the Lord."

Sometimes, however, we find it difficult to really trust God to take care of our problems. That's where the second step comes in. Psalm 37 instructs us to commit our ways (or, in this case, our problems) to the Lord; then it immediately tells us to trust Him to take care of them.

"It is usually at this point that I find Satan whispering his little lies in my ear," Betty said, "such as, 'That's too minor to bother the Lord with. Why don't you just handle this one yourself?' or, 'Who do you think you are that you can ask God to do that for you? Do you really think He cares about that?' or, 'What if the Lord doesn't work it out the way you want?' The doubts and fears crop up immediately."

What does Betty do? "By an act of faith, not feelings, I simply reply, 'Thank You, Lord, for I know You are taking care of my problem. Lord, I believe. Help my unbelief.'"

Remember the man who came to Jesus, asking that his son be healed? Jesus asked the man if he believed that Jesus could heal his son. The man's honest response was, "I do believe; help me overcome my unbelief" (Mark 9:24, NIV). That is the essence of trust.

The next step is delighting in the Lord, praising Him and thanking Him for what He can and will do. To help remember the steps of this prayer of thanks, you can use this acrostic made with the letters of the word *delight:*

> Daily
> Everything
> Laid
> Into
> God's
> Hands
> Totally

Daily, everything laid into God's hands totally! Repeating this phrase helps us remember to keep ourselves committed to the Lord. Then we are able to move on to the fourth step, rest.

"Be still before the Lord." *Rest!* Everything is centered in the Lord. It is not in our power or control. We commit our problems to the Lord, we trust the Lord, we delight in the Lord, and finally we are able to rest in the Lord. "Committing, trusting, delighting, and resting are the only ways

I have been able to survive the painful parts of life," Jan says.

"I have used this process for over twenty years now; it has been the keystone to my emotional health," Betty said. "When I'm in the middle of a problem, I may not understand His answer. But I can always look back and say without doubt that everything I have ever relinquished to the Lord and left in His hands has turned out far better than if I had taken things into my own hands and tried to make them work out my way."

## Other Types of Prayer

There are times when our children and grandchildren are downright irritating. Perhaps we have quarreled with them, or they may have made choices that have hurt us deeply. Try as we might, we find it very difficult to forgive them. We pray, but we just don't have it in our power to make room in our hearts for that person. This is the time for the carpenter's prayer: "Jesus, I know You are a carpenter. I give You permission to build a room in my heart for this person." As you pray this prayer, give up any preconceived ideas of changing the other person to be the way you think he or she should be. Give God permission to make the changes within *you,* and watch as He makes a room in your heart for that person.

One grandma told us, "I never stop praying for my ex–son-in-law. Long ago, when he married my daughter, I made a room for him in my heart and it will be there forever."

"I pray for everyone who was ever a part of my family," Jan added. "Long ago, I made a room for those people in my heart, and it will be there forever. My prayers are with everyone who is now a part of my grandchildren's family."

Sometimes, however, we must make choices and take action. Several courses are open, all of which seem good. In such cases, we pray the "increase-decrease" prayer. We simply say, "Father, if I am to do this, then increase the desire within me to do it. If I am not to do it, then decrease the desire within me."

Betty says she has used this prayer frequently when she has wondered if she should "help" her children or grandchildren. "I also used it when I was trying to decide whether or not to write this book," she said. "Often the increase-decrease prayer may not work instantly, but if I leave it with God, I either keep thinking about that particular action or I forget it."

Sometimes particular situations or problems are so overwhelming that no matter how much we commit them to the Lord, we still find them constantly on our minds. When that happens, ask the Lord to bring to your mind, or to help you find, a verse of Scripture to anchor your thoughts.

"When our youngest daughter, Kristi, was in a disastrous relationship with a young man, the Lord reminded me of Jeremiah 29:11: ' "For I know the plans I have for you," declares the LORD, "plans to prosper you and not to harm you, plans to give you hope and a future" ' (NIV). I knew I had prayed very hard about this relationship," Betty recalled. "I also knew I had done everything within my power to break it up. I knew, intellectually, that God cared even more about Kristi than I did, yet emotionally I was torn up inside. All my waking thoughts were on this bad situation. It was literally eating me up. I was finally able to really let go and leave it committed to the Lord when I began to repeat that Scripture verse every time Kristi came to my mind."

That verse from Jeremiah is important to Jan too. "I like

to personalize it with the names of my children, my children-in-law, and my grandchildren," she said. When one of her sons was going through a particularly hard decision-making time in his life, she often said this prayer: " 'I know the plans I have for you, _____ (inserting the name),' declares the Lord, 'plans to prosper you and not to harm you, plans to give you hope and a future.' "

Now as Jan looks back on it, she realizes "what wonderful hope that brought to me, a mom who would have loved to jump right in and tell my son what to do. Scripture gives that objectivity and heavenly perspective we can get in no other way."

Another simple relinquishment prayer is the soaking prayer. Picture God's love as a pool of blessing. Bring people to that pool, watch them enter it and become submerged, then leave them there to absorb His love.

Jan said, "I pray that God will fill Michelle and Colleen's rooms with His presence as they sleep and that they will be soaked with His love. I often use this prayer at night, just before I go to sleep. It allows me to sleep in peace."

Sometimes when we sit down to pray for our grandchildren, we find that all kinds of thoughts and noises bombard us. The more we try to shut them out, the more they intrude. Betty discovered a simple way to handle those distractions. "When the leaf-blower is roaring in my ears, I simply say, 'Lord, bless the gardener and his family.' If an airplane is flying overhead, rattling the windows, I thank the Lord for the skills of the pilot and ask God to bless him and his passengers and bring them safely home. As soon as I bless the noises, I find I can tune them out.

"It works with my thoughts too. I find they are like children—the more I try to ignore them, the more they hang around and pester me. So I try to spiritualize them. For instance, if I sit down to pray and suddenly remember that I need to take out the garbage, I say, 'Lord, please remove all the garbage from my life.' If I remember that I haven't watered my plants, I may say, 'Lord, water me with Your Word.'"

The Bible is crucial to prayer. The degree to which you believe in God's Word and apply it to your prayer time determines the degree to which God will pour out His power during your prayers. Through using and learning God's Word, you will begin to understand how much power God has made available to you.

In no other way is your faith as strengthened. How can any of us claim God's promises unless we know what they are? Your prayer time, no matter how intense, is never truly complete without the divine nourishment available only from God's Word.

Here are some suggestions for using Scripture in your prayer time:

## A Psalm of Praise: Psalm 8

After you read this psalm of praise, you might want to adapt it to your family, inserting the names of your children or grandchildren in this way:

*I thank You, God, for Your majestic creation in my family. I acknowledge that _____ (names of your grandchildren) are gifts from Your hand. They are the works of Your fingers, as are the moon and stars. You have set them into my life because You are mindful of me. Let me see Your glory in them and how You have crowned them also*

*with glory and honor. Let me see Your love in
_____ (grandchildren's names), and
how that love can be lived out through them.*

*Thank You, God, for giving me to them. Let me be
Your channel to do Your work in them. O Lord, our
Lord, how majestic is Your name in all the earth!
Amen.*

## A Prayer of Trust: Psalm 131

After reading this psalm of trust, you might make it into
a prayer about releasing your worry about your grandchildren:

*O God, I do not concern myself about the things I
place in Your hands. I keep my mind quiet and
think on Your peace. I struggle to leave my concerns
about _____ (name specific concerns
here) there. But again and again I put my hope in
You alone. Amen.*

## The Lord's Prayer: Matthew 6:9–13

After reading, or reciting, the Lord's Prayer, try writing
your own prayer to your heavenly Father. It might go
something like this:

*Our Father in heaven, I honor Your name.
I anxiously await Your coming.
I long for Your will to be done in me and in
_____ (names of your grandchildren)
here on earth as it is in heaven.
Meet my needs today for wisdom and strength.
Help me to learn the way of forgiveness.*

*Keep me on Your way. Lead _____
(your grandchildren) to it.*

*Cover us with Your mighty wings, a shield against
the evil one.*

*I acknowledge that all power and glory are Yours,
forever and ever.*

*Amen.*

## Paul's Prayer for a Deeper Faith: Ephesians 3:14–19

After reading Paul's prayer for a deeper faith, you can write your own prayer for a closer walk with God:

*Father, I acknowledge that You are over all of
heaven and earth. Strengthen me with the power of
Your Holy Spirit so that Christ may dwell in my
heart. Root my grandchildren _____
(name your grandchildren) and me in faith and love
so that we may be stable in Your love and have Your
power, and so that we may begin to understand how
deep is the love of Christ. As we know Your love may
we be changed and filled full of Yourself! Amen.*

### An Hour a Day for Change

Have you ever thought of giving your grandchildren a daily gift of your time in prayer? Not just a few spare minutes here and there, but a substantial gift? We know, we know. You are already so busy you don't see how you could possibly squeeze in such a commitment. But if prayer does indeed work, if it does move the muscles of God's omnipotent arm, then isn't it worth a serious effort to pray for those you love? Start with a few minutes and work up from there. The important thing is to start with a commitment to do it.

Most of us pray a specific prayer, receive an answer—which may or may not be to our liking—and consider the case closed. That's not how God does it. Evelyn Christenson, in her book *What Happens When Women Pray,* suggests that while we are saying "case closed," He is opening up a whole new arena of action. A more appropriate conclusion to our prayer, she suggests, would be to say, "What's next, Lord?"

Jeremiah 33:3 tells us, "Call to me and I will answer you and tell you great and unsearchable things you do not know" (NIV).

Have you ever thought how incredible it would be if you could get a glimpse into God's mind? Well, there is a way. You can catch that glimpse by examining His answers to your prayers.

The thing that constantly amazes us is that God doesn't limit His answers to what we ask. Jeremiah refers to things we don't even know about, things beyond our limited ideas and plans.

We have talked throughout this book about many things we grandmothers can do for our grandchildren. But of all these, the most wonderful is to learn to pray for them in a manner that will move the muscle of God on their behalf. When we achieve this, God will answer our prayers.

After awakening scared one night, Michelle told Jan, "I wish you could be under my bed, Grandma, so I could just call for you." What a great opportunity it was for Jan to remind Michelle that Grandma's prayers were always with her, asking God to watch over her.

Worried about your grandchildren? Concerned that you cannot be all they need you to be? Frustrated because you can't see them as often as you would like? Anxious about the world in which they are growing up? So are we. There's only one answer: to commit our grandchildren to God: "Now to him who is able to do immeasurably more than all we ask or imagine, according to his power that is at work within us" (Eph. 3:20 NIV).

### Grandma's Prayers Make a Difference

When Betty visited Saint Petersburg, Russia, in the summer of 1992, she was repeatedly struck by the changes that had occurred since she visited there in 1973 (when the city was called Leningrad). Back then she had visited museums that, before the days of communism, had been beautiful cathedrals. "The Museum of Atheism and Religion was especially appalling," Betty recalled. "In the basement, there were rooms filled with scenes depicting cruelty and torture perpetrated in the name of Christ during the Crusades and the Inquisition. There were other scenes mocking Christianity, such as mock cathedrals constructed out of bombs and labeled 'The Cathedral of Capitalism.'"

Betty recalled trying to talk about God and Jesus Christ to the well-educated young guide in charge of their 1973 tour. Finally, in frustration, the young lady said, "You just don't understand. When we have been raised and indoctrinated in atheism since birth, we just can't believe any other way."

Almost twenty years later Betty returned to that museum. "Imagine our shock when we found the entire basement empty and closed off!" Betty said. "All the scenes were dismantled, and upstairs in the main sanctuary, where there had been especially mocking displays, religious icons and relics were now being reverently shown."

Picking up on their interest in religion, their guide—a

young Russian schoolteacher—took them to visit Saint Nicholas Cathedral, the only church in the city that had remained open during the seventy years of communism. As they entered, they noticed a hundred or so older women praying in the sanctuary. But what impressed Betty most was the guide's story:

During World War II, Leningrad was under siege by the Germans for three years. During that entire time, Saint Nicholas Cathedral was open every day except for two weeks. "And my grandmother came here almost every day," the guide said, adding that thousands of people died of starvation in those terrible years, including nine of her grandmother's ten children.

"Why did my grandmother and mother live? They said it was because of their faith in God," the guide reported. Since things have changed in Russia, this young man has been baptized and worships regularly at Saint Nicholas. "I had a praying grandma," he said with pride.

As Betty left, she looked again at the faithful older women and was struck with the importance of their prayers. In spite of everything the government could do to wipe out their faith, they had remained faithful.

From there, Betty's group went to Saint Isaac's, a beautiful cathedral with pillars of lapis, malachite, and marble. The gold inscriptions that encircled the dome and crossed underneath the magnificently painted walls were Scripture verses that clearly proclaimed God and His salvation. The young guide in Saint Isaac's told them this cathedral would soon be reopened as a church, and she added that she was anxious for this to happen. "My grandmother always worshiped God here," she said, "and my mother and I are waiting to be baptized."

Two young people, raised and educated in a totally atheistic state, carefully chosen and trained as government employees, painstakingly screened before being allowed to speak with English-speaking visitors, and both were anxious to share their excitement and anticipation of becoming part of the community of faith. Why? We believe it was because of the prayers of their grandmothers.

As with the Russian grandmas' prayers, changes often come gradually, both in our grandchildren and in ourselves. In our experiences, answers take a lot longer than we want them to. But the time and persistence are ever so worthwhile. The rewards are great. We guarantee it!

Grandma, you *do* make a difference!